# The A to Z of Mod

# The A to Z of Mod

**Paolo Hewitt and Mark Baxter**
**Foreword by Martin Freeman**

PRESTEL
MUNICH · LONDON · NEW YORK

# Contents

| | | | |
|---|---|---|---|
| Foreword | 6 | The Creation | 94 |
| Introduction | 10 | DC Fontana | 96 |
| *Absolute Beginners* | 14 | Julie Driscoll | 100 |
| Acid Jazz Records | 18 | Roger Eagle | 102 |
| The Action | 22 | The Eyes | 106 |
| Amphetamine | 24 | Georgie Fame | 108 |
| Atlantic Records | 26 | Fanzines | 112 |
| Austin's Clothes Shop | 30 | Fleur De Lys | 116 |
| Baracuta's G-9 Jacket | 32 | Martin Freeman | 118 |
| Bass Weejuns | 36 | Galliano | 120 |
| Blue Note Records | 38 | Glam Rock and Pub Rock | 122 |
| The Blues | 42 | Dave Godin | 128 |
| Books | 46 | Hair | 132 |
| Britpop | 48 | Irish Jack | 136 |
| Brooks Brothers | 54 | The Isle of Wight Scooter Rally | 138 |
| Cinema | 56 | The Ivy Shop | 140 |
| Eric Clapton | 62 | Jazz Style | 144 |
| Clarks Desert Boots | 66 | Jump the Gun | 148 |
| Clubs Past | 70 | Kent Records | 152 |
| Clubs Present | 80 | Levi's Jeans | 154 |
| Randy Cozens | 86 | | |

Legendary British jazz drummer
Phil Seamen lost in the moment

| | | | |
|---|---|---|---|
| Cathy McGowan | 158 | The Small Faces | 236 |
| Pete Meaden | 162 | Stax Records | 242 |
| Modern Jazz Quartet | 168 | John Stephen | 250 |
| Mohair | 172 | Stone Foundation | 256 |
| Motown | 174 | James Taylor Quartet | 258 |
| Northern Soul | 180 | Tootal Scarves | 260 |
| Online Modernism | 184 | Twiggy | 262 |
| Ronan O'Rahilly | 188 | The Union Jack | 266 |
| The Parka | 192 | Justin de Villeneuve | 270 |
| Peckham Rye | 196 | Paul Weller | 272 |
| Fred Perry | 198 | The Who | 280 |
| Pop Art | 202 | Bradley Wiggins | 284 |
| *Quadrophenia – The Film* | 206 | Generation X | 288 |
| | | The Yardbirds | 290 |
| Mary Quant | 210 | Young Disciples | 292 |
| *Ready, Steady, Go!* | 214 | Zoot Money | 294 |
| Revival | 218 | Acknowledgements and Credits | 296 |
| Rickenbacker Guitars | 224 | | |
| The Roundel | 228 | | |
| The Scooter | 230 | | |
| Ben Sherman | 234 | | |

# Foreword

The comedian Lenny Bruce had a bit where he listed various people, things and places as being 'Jewish' or 'goyish'. As memory serves, the first group included Ray Charles and Count Basie, the second white bread. The implication was that one group, 'Jewish', was soulful, authentic, complex. The goys, I'm afraid, were plastic, trivial.

Well, substitute 'Jewish' for 'Mod', and I think you'll have a fair idea of what this book, this code, this thing of ours is about.

There are many people, songs, paintings, films, books, motor vehicles, even coffee bars that would not see themselves or be seen by their creators as 'Mod', any more than Count Basie was Jewish. Did any of the writers, producers or singers of the thousands of obscure Northern Soul tunes that we love think of themselves as Mods? Nope. They weren't even making 'Northern Soul'. Do Peter Blake or Bridget Riley consider themselves Faces? Did Truffaut or Godard?

Well, no.

But somehow, they *are*.

That, to me, is part of the Mod genius. Having great taste. Knowing where to look and, more importantly, what to look for.

Dance music that you won't hear on the radio but which will blow your mind and burst your heart? Art that is about now, in the language of pop culture? Cinema that has to be sought out, in that sense elitist, and still looks heartbreakingly cool? Check, check, check.

Cut to 50 years later.

Each new wave of people who have identified themselves with Modernism have had something new to bring to the party. New clothes, music, moves, details. I think the basic influences, from the originals, stay pretty firm. But they didn't wear Gazelles. Nor had they been through punk. Or (and I'm with Il Scrivo here) hip hop. The barnets currently seen on Messrs Weller and Gallagher are absolutely Mod, but '64 at The Flamingo they ain't.

It develops. It moves on. When it doesn't, it's fancy dress. Costume. It's Dressing Like A Mod. And that's not for me, brother.

It's also personal. And not easily understood. Many's the time I've had people question my sanity over things I've worn, records I've bought, moves I've made. As with belief of any kind, it requires and engenders commitment. That can be a lonely road. That's why when we identify a brother or sister, our hearts beat faster; we want to share music, coffee and talk about shoes. Not that we usually do that. A quick nod tells the other that we understand, and serves as the all-purpose stylist salute.

Above all, I think Mod is a rejection of the obvious. The authors of this book recognise that, and have included entries that will inform as well as confirm. They themselves have pretty eclectic tastes in matters of weft and wax, and can hold forth on loving The Fabs, or the joy of an obscure detail of a shirt cuff from October – no, *December* '66. Not obscurity for its own sake, which is deeply tedious, but a recognition that we can do better if we make the effort, dammit. It's not a uniform, it's the (highest) common denominator.

So enjoy reading about the genesis of your favourite shoes. Or be outraged at the omission of the best underground Freakbeat/psych B-side you've ever heard.

As long as we keep caring.

The world thinks we're mad anyway.

Martin Freeman
New Zealand, 2012

# Introduction

Mod moves in mysterious ways and so it is right and proper that its birthday, its history, is still somewhat shrouded in mystery. For me, Mod began in 1958 and ended in 1963. For others it was the opening of the Club Eleven on Soho's Great Windmill Street in the late 1940s that acted as the catalyst for Mod. Some will argue that Mod means Carnaby Street and Union Jack jackets, others will point to coffee bars and jazz. I would consider the novel *American Psycho* by Bret Easton Ellis a Mod book and Martin Scorsese's *Mean Streets* a Mod film. I always thought the hip hop and acid house scenes were totally Mod. Others think I must be pilled out of my head to make such assertions. Mod defies all categorisation and so it should: that is one of its great strengths. What is certain is that Mod has flourished for over 50 years now and shows no sign of abating. That idea of creating a world within a world, based around cool clothes, music and attitude – of dressing smartly or in a unique way to remove oneself from the herd and then aligning this style with a music that makes you dance to keep from crying – still holds as strong as ever. That is why in this book we have sought to cover all aspects of Britain's greatest youth movement, from Miles Davis to Colin MacInnes to Bradley Wiggins, from Pete Meaden to Acid Jazz to Stone Foundation, with fanzines, films, clothes and books also taking centre stage. W is for the work we have put in, and H is for – we hope you really dig this book.

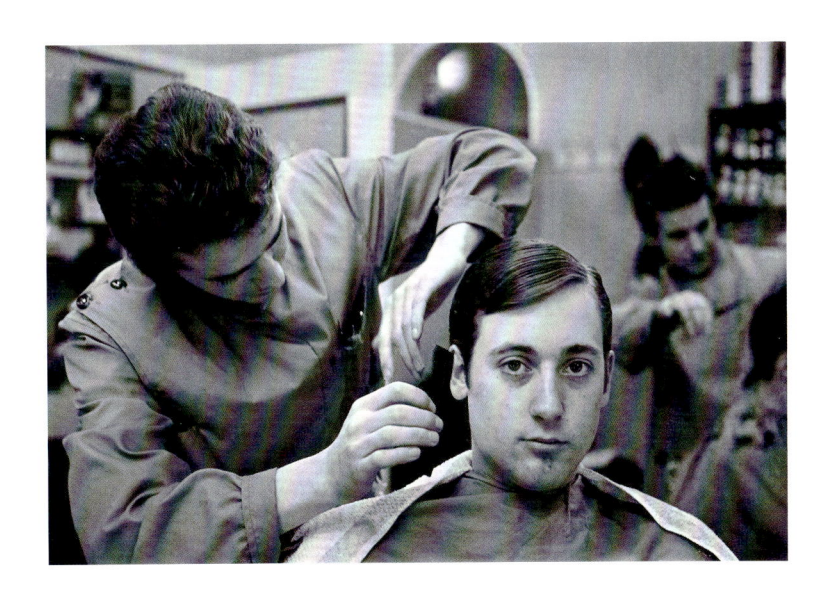

Paolo Hewitt
White Hart Lane, 2012

An Oxbridge teenager getting a university haircut, 1966

A young Mod couple getting
it all right on the back of a
Lambretta in 1963

I first became aware of the world of Mod through a combination of the film *Quadrophenia* and the group The Jam in 1979. After being exposed to the music and the imagery I was hooked. I began to dress the part and not only bought the music of the period, but also began digging back into a pile of classic 45s owned by an uncle of mine. There I found music from The Who to Wilson Pickett and all the stops in between. I found the history of the movement fascinating and still do, hence this book. The word 'Mod' conjures up different things for different people and that is part of its long-lasting appeal. There is something for everyone here.

    I hope you enjoy reading this book as much as I did researching and co-writing it.

Mark Baxter
The Den, 2012

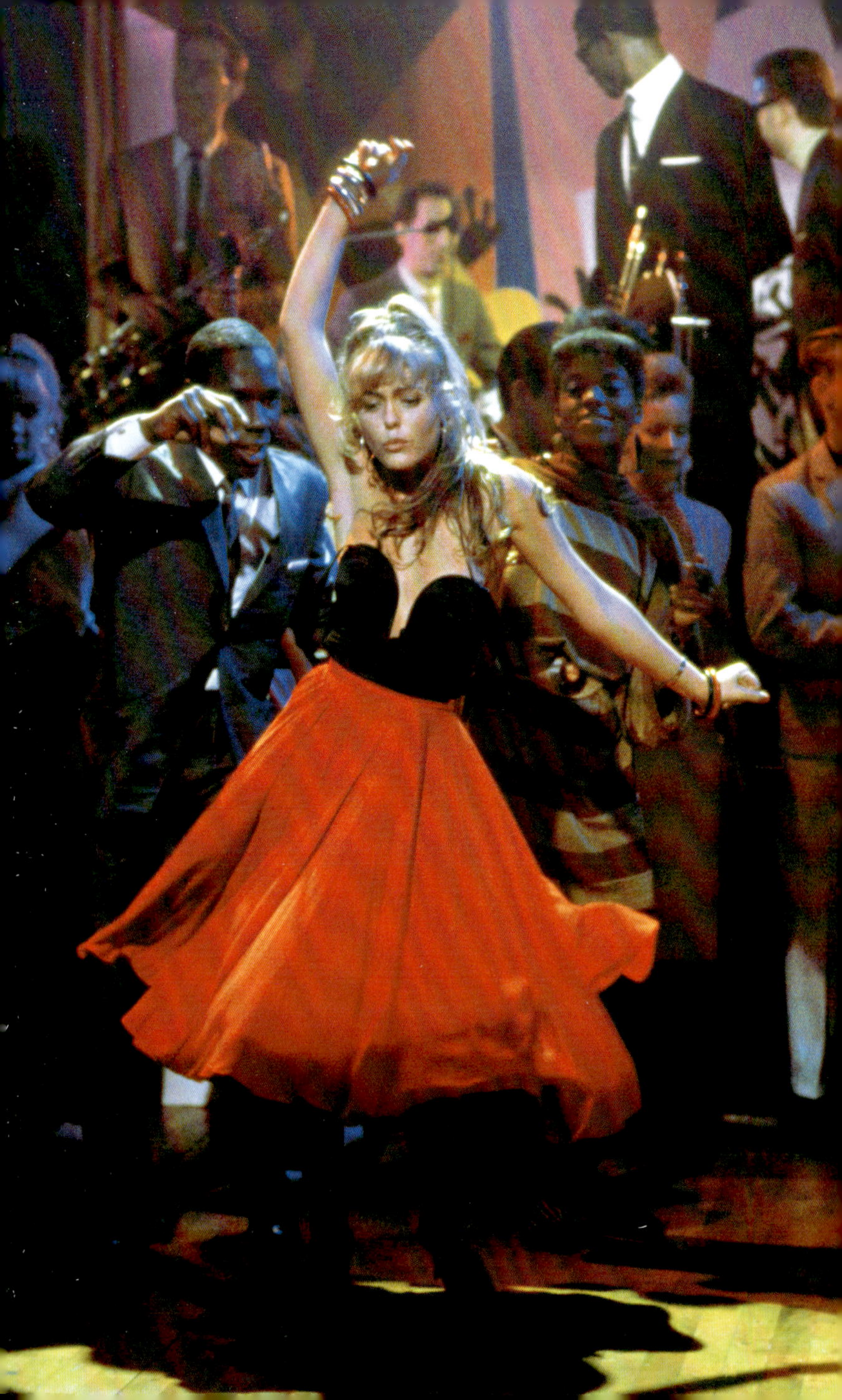

# *Absolute Beginners*

Written by Colin MacInnes in 1959, and published over the years with covers featuring the work of photographer Roger Mayne and artist Peter Blake, *Absolute Beginners* provides an invaluable insight into the origins of the world of Mod. Set in 1958, this key novel follows a Modernist who works as a freelance photographer and inhabits a world made up of coffee bars, scooters and modern jazz. Through the adventures of our unnamed hero, the novel explores many themes, not least that of the teenager's urgent desire to break from staid, boring Britain and build a much hipper and freer world. Racism, the 1958 Notting Hill riots and the contributions of the Caribbean community to London are also detailed.

During the writing and researching of this book, MacInnes lived on Soho's D'Arblay Street and visited Ronnie Scott's jazz club many times. Consequently, his eye for the clothing detail and the language of the young hipsters he

*Opposite:* Actress Patsy Kensit as 'Crepe Suzette' in the 1986 film *Absolute Beginners*

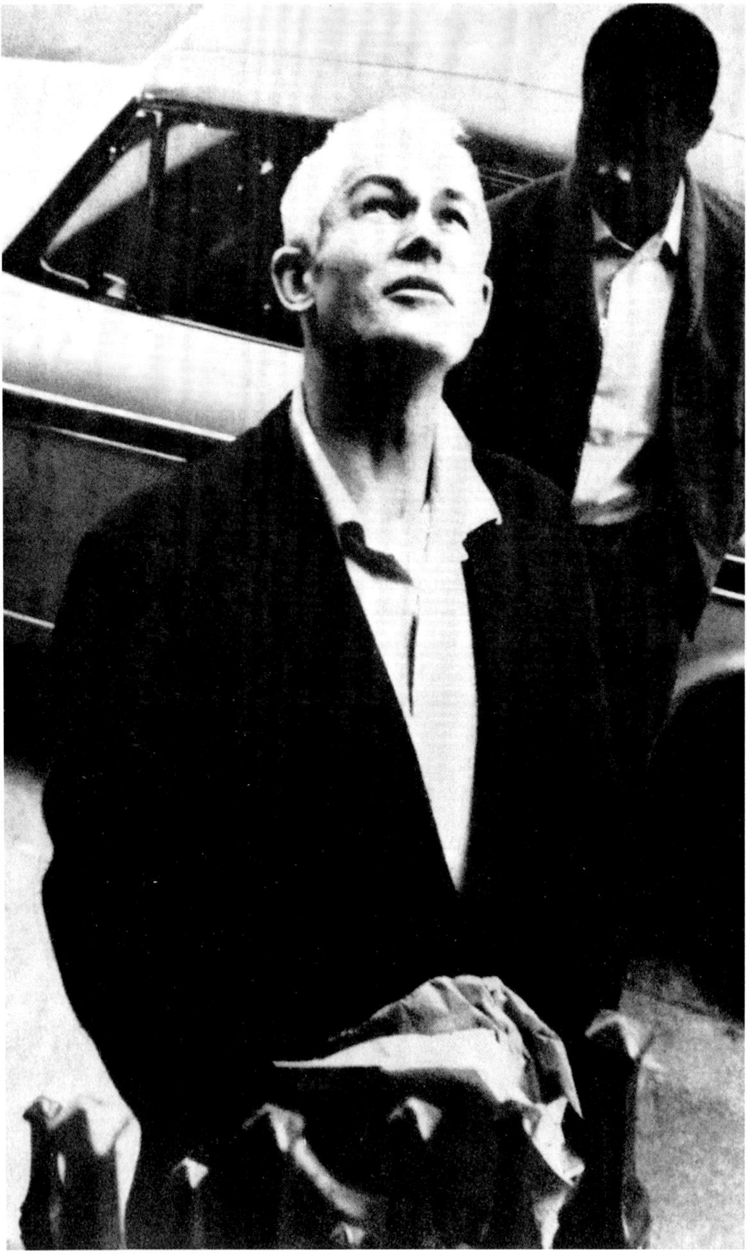

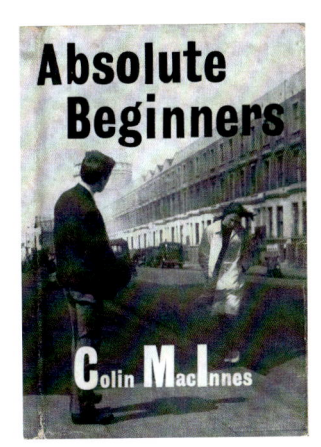

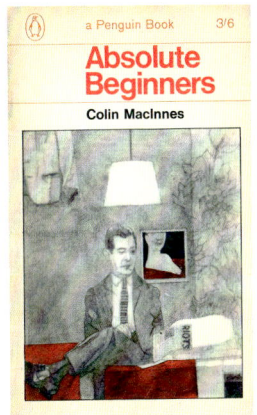

encountered is spot on, as is his understanding of the Mod mind set. The second of a trilogy of London books by MacInnes (the other titles are *City of Spades* and *Mr Love and Justice*), *Absolute Beginners* was adapted to film by Julien Temple in 1986 and starred David Bowie and Patsy Kensit.

*Opposite:* Writer Colin MacInnes

*Left:* The original book jacket with photography by Roger Mayne

*Right:* The 1964 Penguin reissue with a cover designed by Peter Blake

# ACID JAZZ NEWS

- QUENTIN TARANTINO
- ROY AYERS' FANTASY
- NAOMI CAMPBELL
- JACQUI DIXON AT LAST
- NEWS AND REVIEWS

## Brand New Heavies
*Back In The Day*

ISSUE **13** WINTER

**FREE**

# Acid Jazz Records

In 1987 influential radio and club DJ Gilles Peterson teamed up with second-generation Mod-about-town Eddie Piller to form Acid Jazz Records. Fellow DJ Chris Bangs is credited with coming up with the phrase 'acid jazz', a play on the highly popular acid house music that was starting to take off at that time. Acid Jazz Records sought to sign musically interesting acts who were also clothes-conscious, and many well-known musicians got their start at the label, including Galliano, Jamiroquai, The Brand New Heavies, Mother Earth and Corduroy. When Paul Weller wished to release a funk track under the name 'King Truman', it was Acid Jazz the Modfather approached. The label also published the definitive Small Faces biography, *Small Faces: The Young Mods' Forgotten Story* by Paolo Hewitt. Piller's mother, Fran, had been the band's fan club secretary back in the 1960s. Peterson left the operation in 1989 and despite challenging

*Opposite:* Cover of *Acid Jazz News* (Winter 1994) featuring The Brand New Heavies

*Top:* The classic Acid Jazz logo

*Top:* Cover of *Acid Jazz News* (Summer 1995) featuring Mother Earth

*Bottom:* An Acid Jazz flyer

economic conditions, Piller has managed to keep the label afloat. Modwise, the label is testament to Piller's ability to apply Mod sensibilities within a contemporary framework. The man knows his past (witness the label's sought-after *Rare Mod* compilations) but keeps his eye on the present. Thus he has recently released a new album by the veteran singer Tony Christie and signed the Janice Graham Band and The Broken Vinyl Club.

Might as well jump: the band Corduroy in full flight

# The Action

Originally named The Boys, The Action came together in North London in 1963. One of their first gigs was backing singer Sandra Barry. In 1965 they struck out on their own. With Reg King on vocals, Alan 'Bam' King on rhythm guitar, Mike 'Ace' Evans on bass, Peter Watson on lead guitar and Roger Powell on drums, their energetic live performances and stylish image soon attracted a dedicated Mod following. A lot of their success was due to King's vocal prowess. Many now consider him one of the finest ever 'blue-eyed' soul singers. His commanding voice was best heard on The Action's great cover versions of Motown classics such as 'In My Lonely Room', 'Since I Lost My Baby' and 'I'll Keep Holding On'. In 1965 George Martin, producer of The Beatles, signed them to Parlophone Records but despite their many fans on the live circuit, chart success was to elude them. In 1967 they began writing and recording their own material, including their

*Top:* Album cover of The Action's compilation *Uptight and Outasight*, 2004

*Bottom:* Album cover of the compilation *The Ultimate Action*, 1980

landmark songs 'Never Ever' and 'Shadows and Reflections'. However, despite smashing the record for crowd attendance at The Marquee Club, Soho, on several occasions, the band were dropped by Parlophone and a disillusioned Reggie King quit the band to pursue a solo career. His former band mates continued as Mighty Baby but soon ran out of steam.

In the late 1970s, thanks mainly to a Paul Weller-backed compilation, The Action were rediscovered by a second generation of Mods. They later reformed for a few Mod rallies and a gig at The 100 Club in 2004. King also guested as a vocalist on producer Andy Lewis's album *The Billion Pound Project*. Sadly, Mike Evans died in January 2010 aged 65 and Reggie King followed him to Mod heaven in October of the same year.

The Action in Germany, 1966. L to R: Alan 'Bam' King, Roger Powell, Pete Watson, Mike Evans, Reg King

# Amphetamine

Otherwise known as speed, amphetamine was the perfect drug for Mods. Its ability to keep the user awake for lengthy periods of time allowed Modernists to literally speed through a whole weekend of clubbing and shopping. The drug was first discovered in 1887 and came into its own during the Second World War when British soldiers used it to fight combat fatigue. At war's end, it became readily available on London's streets. In fact, such was its popularity among the Mod fraternity that top Mod band The Small Faces wrote a celebratory song about it titled 'Here Come the Nice'. In the 1964 BBC *Panorama* documentary on Mods, one pill popper shocked the nation by casually admitting to taking something like 30 pills over a weekend. Amphetamine's high usage eventually attracted front-page headlines, which in turn prompted police raids on many Mod clubs.

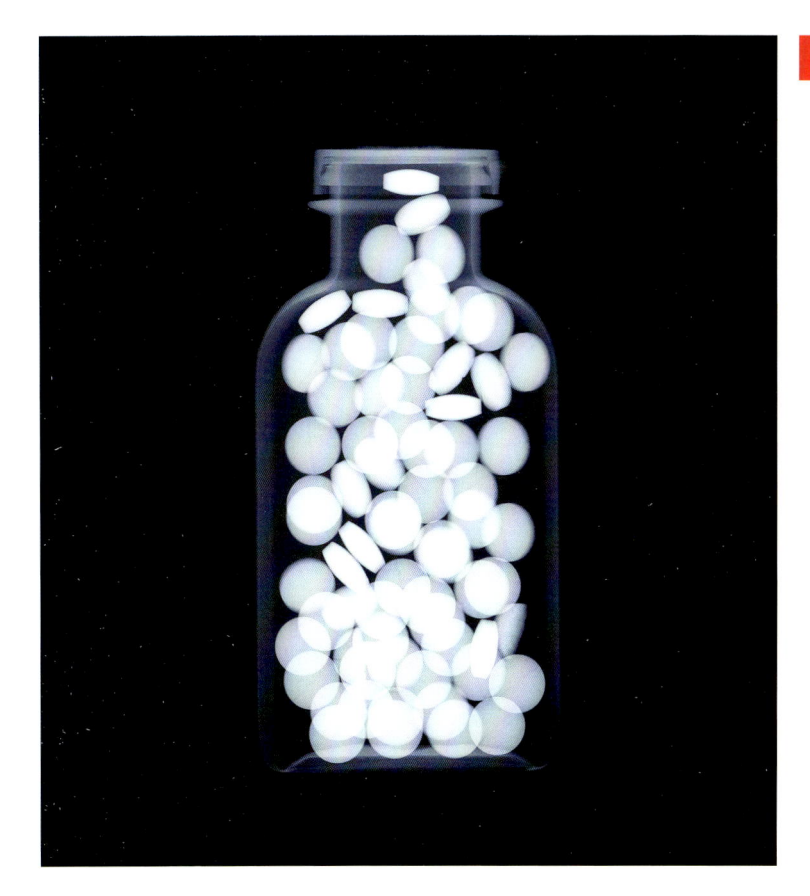

Other sobriquets for the drug include Blues, Bennies, Purple Hearts and Dexys. The last two names were appropriated by groups, The Purple Hearts and Dexys Midnight Runners. In the 1970s the drug was popular in the growing Northern Soul scene.

In the UK speed is classified as a Class B drug. Side effects include dilated pupils, a dry mouth and insomnia, and the 'come down' can include deep mental fatigue and high anxiety, as many Mods will testify.

Here come the nice: X-ray of a bottle of pills

Nesuhi Ertegun (C), President of Atlantic Records, with Vice Presidents Jerry Wexler (L) and Ahmet Ertegun (R)

# Atlantic Records

Founded in New York City in 1947 by Ahmet Ertegun and Herb Abramson (with a $10,000 loan from Ertegun's dentist), the music of Atlantic acts such as Ray Charles, Ruth Brown, Aretha Franklin, Otis Redding, Wilson Pickett, The Rascals, Solomon Burke, John Coltrane and Charles Mingus, to name but a few, has always been highly regarded and revered by Mods past and present. Through the guidance of producer and A&R man Jerry Wexler, Atlantic Records placed itself at the heart of American black music for many years, whether blues, jazz or soul. Key records among a sea of many would include Doris Troy's 'Whatcha Gonna Do About It', Joe Tex's 'Hold What You Got', Solomon Burke's 'Everybody Needs Somebody to Love', Don Covay's 'Mercy Mercy', Deon Jackson's 'Love Makes the World Go Round' and John Coltrane's 'Olé', a nine-minute freeform jazz instrumental that was often played at The Scene Club,

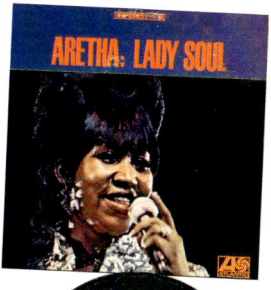

*Top:* Album cover of *Lady Soul* by Aretha Franklin, 1968

*Bottom:* Centre of the 45 rpm single 'Rock Steady' by Aretha Franklin according to regular attendee Alfie Wyatt. Atlantic also brought the famous Stax label (see Stax Records) under its umbrella, while famously unleashing the incredible Aretha Franklin on the world in 1967, the same year Warner Brothers bought the company for $17 million. The next year Atlantic signed the rock band Led Zeppelin, signalling the company's highly successful move into rock music. They also later signed The Rolling Stones.

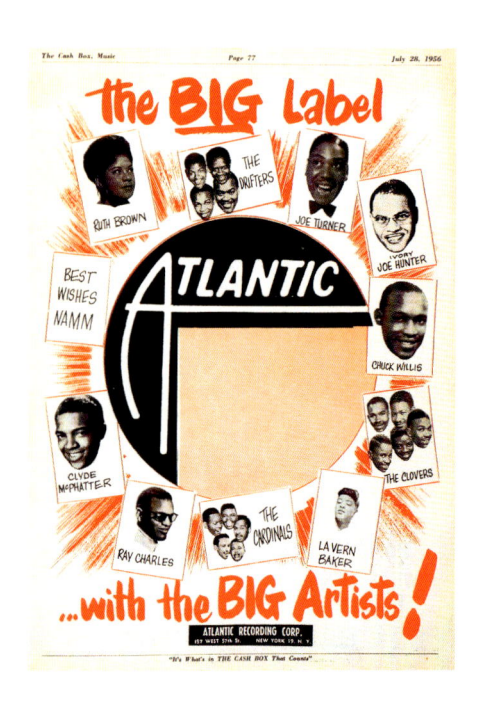

Ahmet Ertegun later co-founded the New York Cosmos soccer team. He died in late 2006 at the age of 83.

Advertisement for recording artists on Atlantic Records, 1950s

Pain in his heart: soul singer Otis Redding giving it plenty in the year of his death, 1967, aged just 26

# Austin's Clothes Shop

Austin Ltd was one of London's first true Modernist shops, a classy operation situated in Piccadilly at the end of Shaftesbury Avenue, opposite the Trocadero. Austin's stocked classic, imported Ivy League clothing such as seersucker jackets, button-down shirts by companies such as Arrow and Enro, and knitwear of every hue. The shop's own range of suits were made by Dougie Millings, who shot to fame later on in life as tailor to The Beatles. Described as having a 'dowdy' interior, the shop window was anything but and the likes of writer Nik Cohn could often be found drooling over the clothing it displayed. Austin's charged top prices for their goods, but the young and obsessed were prepared to pay them. In fact, it is said that Charlie Watts, drummer with The Rolling Stones, would spend almost his entire wages in there on a Friday night. Georgie Fame and a young Eric Clapton, two of London's leading Modernists, were also regular

Magazine advert for Austin's, late 1950s

visitors. The shop was owned by one Louis Austin, a former musician from the 1930s who displayed impeccable Mod instincts by living in a top hotel. The shop survived until the early 1970s.

*Top:* The Yardbirds in 1964. Eric Clapton, far right, is wearing a buttoned-up Baracuta G-9 Harrington (see Baracuta's G-9 Jacket)

*Bottom:* Georgie Fame goes 'three-piece' in 1967

# B

GOD SAVE
THE G9
BARACUTA

# Baracuta's G-9 Jacket

From its humble beginnings in a small factory in Manchester *circa* 1937, the Baracuta G-9 jacket has now become a world-famous, iconic piece of clothing thanks to its classic design and the patronage of stars from Elvis Presley to Liam Gallagher. Moreover, since its launch the jacket has stayed true to its original design.

The Baracuta Clothing Company was started by the brothers John and Isaac Miller in 1937. One of their first moves was to produce a revolutionary design for a blouson jacket. This became the template for the G-9. Once the Scottish Fraser Clan had granted permission for Baracuta to use their tartan as a lining, the jacket was launched to great success. The finances the jacket accrued for Baracuta allowed Isaac Miller to look across the Atlantic to America and open an office in the Empire State Building in New York. When Elvis Presley wore a G-9 in the film *King Creole* in 1958, sales rocketed. In the 1960s the

*Opposite:* The classic Baracuta G-9 complete with Fraser lining; 'God Save The G9 Baracuta' pin badge

*Top:* Advert for Baracuta, 1950s

33

# Advertising to Russian Trade

actor Ryan O'Neal, playing Rodney Harrington in the US television series *Peyton Place*, wore the jacket so much that his character became synonymous with the item. When the clothing entrepreneur John Simons (see The Ivy Shop) began selling the jacket at his shop, located in Richmond, Surrey, he naturally labelled it a Harrington. The name stuck and the Harrington is now a wardrobe staple for those in the know.

Other famous wearers of the jacket include a Yardbirds-era Eric Clapton and the actor Steve McQueen. The G-9 is often copied but there is only one original, and that is the Baracuta.

*Top:* Advert for a Russian trade magazine

*Bottom:* Advert for Baracuta rainwear

*Opposite top:* A selection of Baracuta jackets

*Opposite bottom:* Where it all began: the original Manchester factory

G2 vintage

G3 vintage

Trench coat vintage

G4 vintage

35

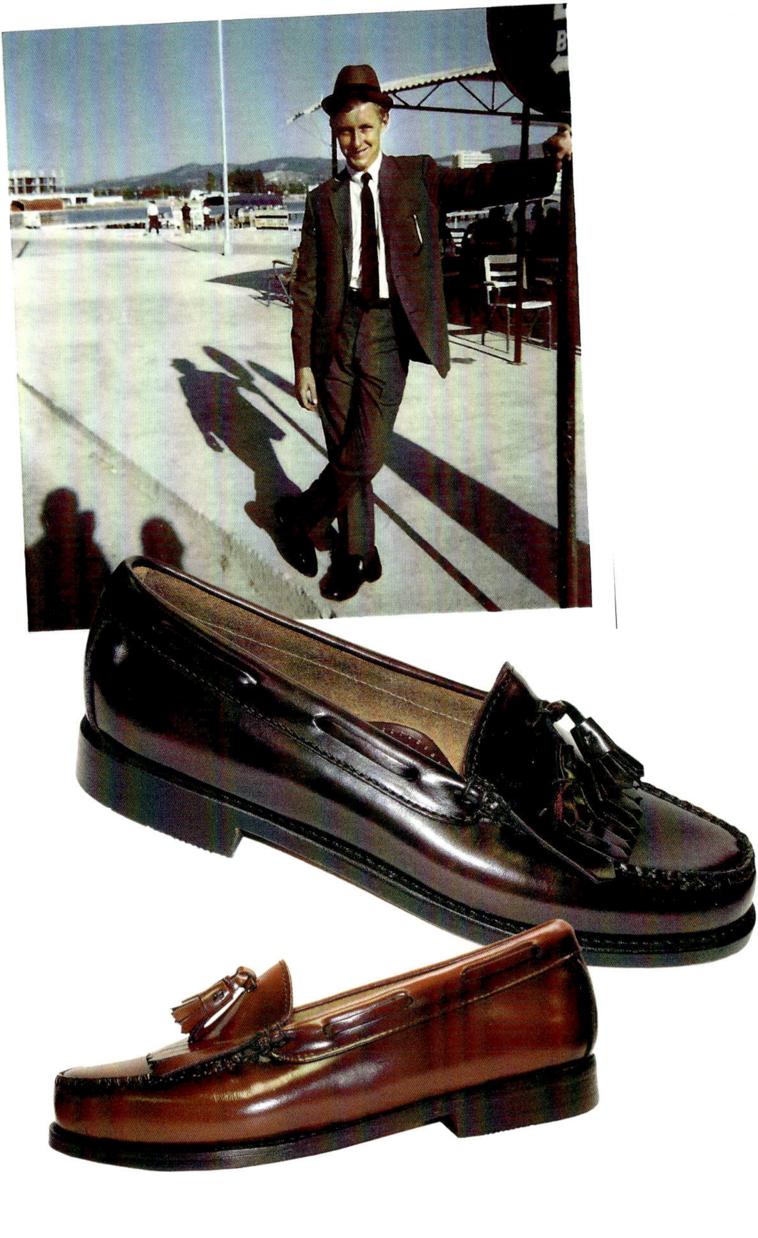

# Bass Weejuns

That trumpet player and stylish dresser Miles Davis swore by Bass Weejuns and was often seen sporting a pair should tell us a hell of a lot about this shoe's high quality. In 1934 the G. H. Bass footwear company of Maine began making a moccasin-style shoe which they named a 'Weejun', a derivation of the word Norwegian. Why this word? Because in the early 1930s *Esquire* magazine had carried photographs of Norwegian farmers wearing a shoe that later inspired the design. This style of casual slip-on shoe became very popular on Ivy League campuses and was later appropriated by London's Modernists, who knew it as a loafer. The various styles of the Bass Weejun are the Beef Roll, the Penny and the Tasselled.

There was a huge resurgence of interest in the shoes in the early to mid-1980s, thanks to bands such as The Style Council, and to this day they remain highly popular.

*Opposite top:* Even on holiday in Spain in 1965, a young Mod had to look his best

*Opposite bottom:* Two fine examples of the fringe and tassel Bass Weejun, the Layton

*Top:* The Bass logo

*Bottom:* The classic Penny Loafer

# THE MIDNIGHT SPECIAL
## will get you there...
### the latest by
### *Jimmy Smith*
### Worlds Greatest Jazz Organist

MIDNIGHT SPECIAL • JIMMY SMITH with Stanley Turrentine, tenor sax; Kenny Burrell, guitar; Donald Bailey, drums • MIDNIGHT SPECIAL, A SUBTLE ONE, JUMPIN' THE BLUES, WHY WAS I BORN, ONE O'CLOCK JUMP
BLUE NOTE 4078°

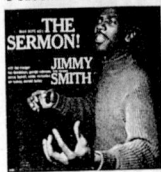

The Sermon  BLP 4011*
Crazy! Baby  BLP 4030*
Home Cookin'  BLP 4050*

WRITE FOR FREE CATALOG  *ALSO AVAILABLE IN STEREO

# BLUE NOTE
43 West 61st Street, New York 23, N. Y.

# Blue Note Records

This is the story of the Lion and the Wolff. In 1938 a jazz-obsessed German named Alfred Lion attended a 'From Spirituals to Swing' concert at New York's Carnegie Hall. Deeply inspired by the music he heard that night, Lion was determined to start his own record label. A year later, using money supplied by the writer Max Margulis, Lion started Blue Note Records. His first recordings were by Albert Ammons and Meade 'Lux' Lewis, both masters of the boogie-woogie piano style. Lion was later joined in his venture by childhood friend and photographer Francis Wolff, who had fled Nazi Germany at the end of 1939. At the time, bebop music was sweeping through many cities.

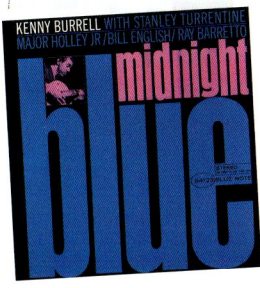

*Opposite:* Blue Note advert from *Down Beat* magazine, December 1961

*Top:* Album cover of *The Congregation* by Johnny Griffin

*Bottom:* The classic album cover of *Midnight Blue* by Kenny Burrell

*Left:* The Blue Note logo

*Left:* Album cover of *Inventions and Dimensions* by Herbie Hancock

*Right:* Album cover of *Cool Struttin'* by Sonny Clark

Yet such was its uncompromising nature that many innovative artists such as Bud Powell, Thelonious Monk and drummer Art Blakey were struggling to find recording contracts. Their music was just too ahead of its time – but not for Blue Note Records. The company fearlessly signed up a whole slew of bebop artists, including Horace Silver, Clifford Brown, Elvin Jones, Kenny Burrell, Jimmy Smith, Lee Morgan, Herbie Hancock, Ornette Coleman, Eric Dolphy and Donald Byrd.

Thanks to Francis Wolff's superb photographs and the brilliant design work of one Reid Miles (who joined the company in 1956), Blue Note music was often presented in highly iconic record sleeves. One thinks of the album sleeves for *Cool Struttin'* by Sonny Clark, *The Congregation* by Johnny Griffin, *Midnight Special* by Jimmy Smith, *Midnight Blue* by Kenny Burrell and Herbie Hancock's *Inventions and*

*Dimensions*. In fact, Modernists would often buy a Blue Note album just for the way it looked and the clothes featured on it.

Bought out by Liberty Records in 1965, Lion and Wolff gradually took a back seat. Their work was done, for at least one classic Blue Note album nestles in the record collection of every discerning Modernist.

A work of art: album cover of *Out to Lunch!* by Eric Dolphy

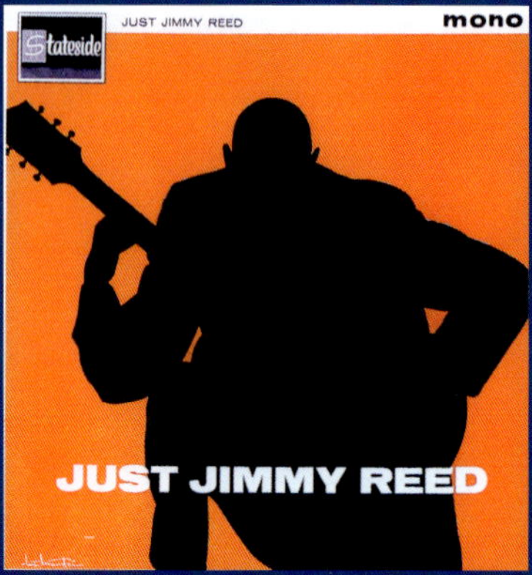
Stateside
JUST JIMMY REED
mono
JUST JIMMY REED

the new jimmy reed album
BLUESWAY
MONAURAL BL-6004

# The Blues

Blues music originates from African-American culture. It was first heard in the fields of the Southern states of the USA, a sound forged from a combination of old spirituals and chants. Many of its lyrics express the tough realities of life experienced by the average African-American worker. The music itself changed when the Great Depression in 1920s America drove many blacks to migrate to major cities such as Chicago and Detroit. This new urban way of life produced a tougher, electric sound which eventually found much favour in Mod clubs. At The Flamingo in Wardour Street, for example, the music played between the live acts was nearly always blues. Meanwhile, acts like Howlin' Wolf, Jimmy Reed and Little Walter, with songs such as 'Smokestack Lightning', 'Key to the Highway' and 'Bright Lights Big City' respectively, were big favourites with Mods. Such was the impact of these blues artists that when they performed in Britain they

*Opposite top left:* Album cover of *Just Jimmy Reed* by Jimmy Reed

*Opposite top right:* Album cover of *The New Jimmy Reed Album* by Jimmy Reed

*Opposite bottom:* British blues great Alexis Korner in a recording studio with his band Blues Incorporated 1963

Blues legend Howlin' Wolf in 1970

were always taken aback by the knowledge and enthusiasm expressed to them by their young, well-dressed audience, most of whom had never set foot in America. Soul was always the Mod's favoured sound but the blues proved to be a wonderful backup.

Little Walter in the mid-1960s

# Books

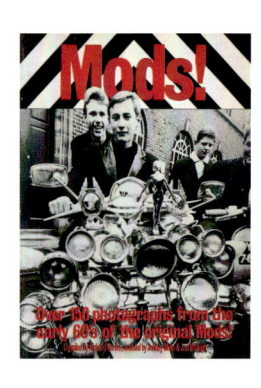

The first book to successfully provide a great overview of the Mod movement was Richard Barnes's 1989 publication, *Mods!*, published – fittingly enough – by Pete Townshend's Eel Pie Publishing. Barnes was an early Mod and lived the life, visiting all the Mod clubs, knowing all the key players, buying all the best clobber. His book exhaustively covers every aspect of the Mod lifestyle, from clothes to records, haircuts to pills. It remains the very best introduction to the scene. Other books of note include Paolo Hewitt's collection of 1960s writings on the subject, *The Sharper Word*. Also worth mentioning is *The Soul Stylists*, his collaboration with Paul Weller which follows the Mod spirit from 1945 to the present day. For a leftfield look at the Mod ethos, Kevin Pearce's *Something Beginning With O* has no contenders, while *The Influential Factor* by Graham Lentz, *Mod: A Very British Phenomenon* by Terry Rawlings

*Mods!* by Richard Barnes

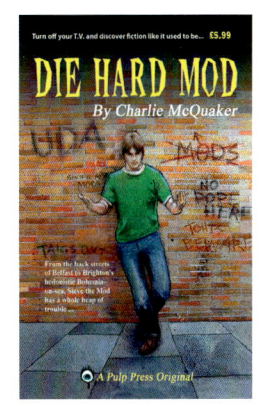

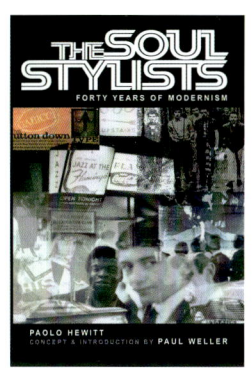

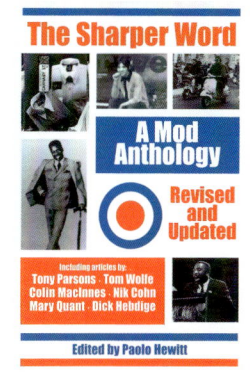

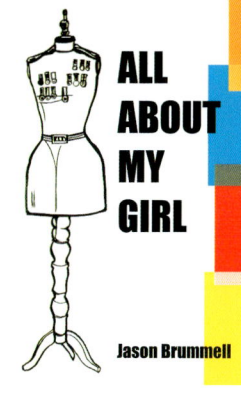

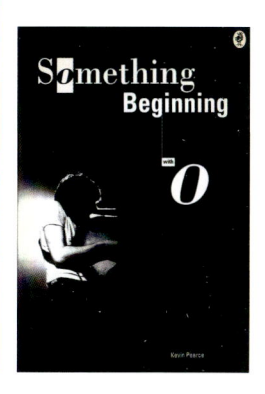

and *The Ivy Look* by Graham Marsh and J. P. Gaul provide great information. Two very good Mod-related books are from the Bee Cool publishing imprint – *The In Crowd* by Mike Ritson and Stuart Russell, a fruitful history of Northern Soul, and *CENtral 1179* by Keith Rylatt and Phil Scott, which concentrates on Manchester's Twisted Wheel club. Fiction-wise, Alan Fletcher's 'Mod Crop' trilogy, *All About My Girl* by Jason Brummell and Charlie McQuaker's *Die Hard Mod* are the leaders in their field.

*Top: Die Hard Mod* by Charlie McQuaker; *The Soul Stylists* by Paolo Hewitt (cover design by Simon Halfon)

*Bottom: The Sharper Word* by Paolo Hewitt (cover design by George Georgiou); *All about my Girl* by Jason Brummell (cover drawing by Nathalie Farrant); *Something Beginning With O* by Kevin Pearce (cover photo by Paul Slattery)

47

The original Oasis line-up: Tony McCarroll, Noel Gallagher, Paul 'Guigsy' McGuigan, Liam Gallagher and Paul 'Bonehead' Arthurs, 1995

# Britpop

For many born in the late 1960s the teenage soundtrack foisted upon them was of little value. Ignoring the New Romantics and the likes of Duran Duran, these music-mad kids either headed backwards to the 1960s or sought out exciting acts such as Happy Mondays and The Stone Roses. Inevitably, Mod touched them in some way, be that through the sound of The Who, The Small Faces or The Jam. The advent of Britpop allowed these bands to use those influences to create a statement, whether that was Noel Gallagher's Union Jack guitar or Steve Cradock's Tootal scarves.

In fact, if there was one band who displayed their Mod influence and heritage proudly, then that was surely Birmingham's Ocean Colour Scene. Formed in 1989 from the wreckage of two local bands, Fanatics and The Boys, OCS comprise guitarist Steve Cradock, bassist Damon Minchella, drummer Oscar Harrison and vocalist

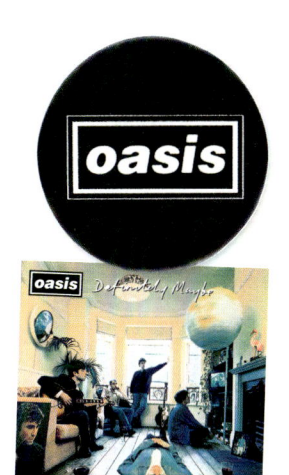

*Top:* The classic black-and-white Oasis logo on a pin badge

*Bottom:* The first Oasis album, the bestselling *Definitely Maybe*, released in 1994

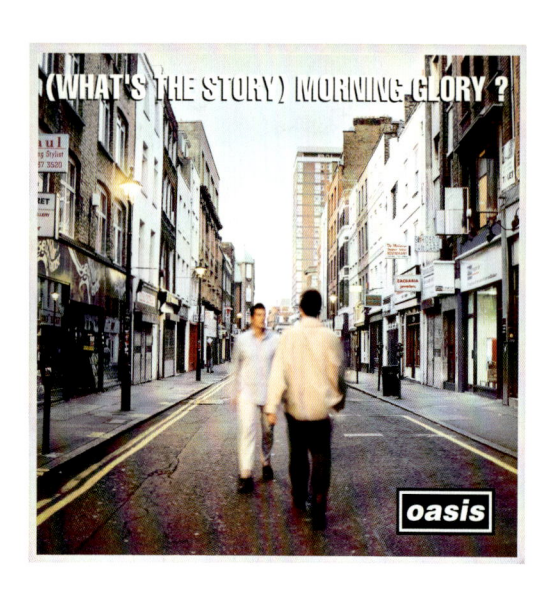

Simon Fowler. Their first single, 'Sway', caught a few people's attention on its release in 1990. The resulting album was produced to fit in with the burgeoning 'Madchester' scene of the time but without the band's permission. Cue a label dispute, which resulted in the band being unable to release any further new music. Meanwhile, OCS had come to the notice of Paul Weller, who remembered being pestered by Cradock at his Solid Bond studios back in the 1980s. Cradock was a huge fan of The Jam and had appropriated a lot of that band's dress, such as bowling shoes and corduroy caps. To his delight, Weller invited OCS to support him on a 1993 UK tour. This in turn led to Cradock playing guitar in Weller's band, where he was later joined by Minchella on bass. Cradock is still there to this day.

An old friendship with the Gallagher brothers from their small club gig circuit days got them a support slot at the legendary Oasis gig at

The cover of the second Oasis album, *(What's The Story) Morning Glory?*, 1995

Manchester City's Maine Road Stadium in 1995, and, having resolved their first recording contract, they signed to MCA Records. Their *Moseley Shoals* album, released in 1996, reached number two in the charts. The four hit singles taken from it, 'The Riverboat Song', 'The Day We Caught the Train', 'You've Got It Bad' and 'The Circle', established a wide audience for the band. The follow-up album *Marchin' Already* (1997) went one better and hit number one. Stadium tours followed, in which the band sold out notable venues such as the Royal Albert Hall. Their use of Mod imagery and culture in both their music and packaging chimed nicely with the advent of the Britpop era.

Minchella left the band in 2003 and guitarists Andy Bennett and Dan Sealey were brought in as replacements. The latest OCS album, *Saturday*, was released in 2010. Steve Cradock released the solo albums *The Kundalini Target*

The original line-up of Ocean Colour Scene. L to R: Simon Fowler, Oscar Harrison, Steve Cradock and Damon Minchella, 1997 and *Peace City West* to critical acclaim in 2009 and 2011 respectively. March 2011 saw the release of a 15th-anniversary special edition of *Moseley Shoals*, supported by a full tour of the UK by the band.

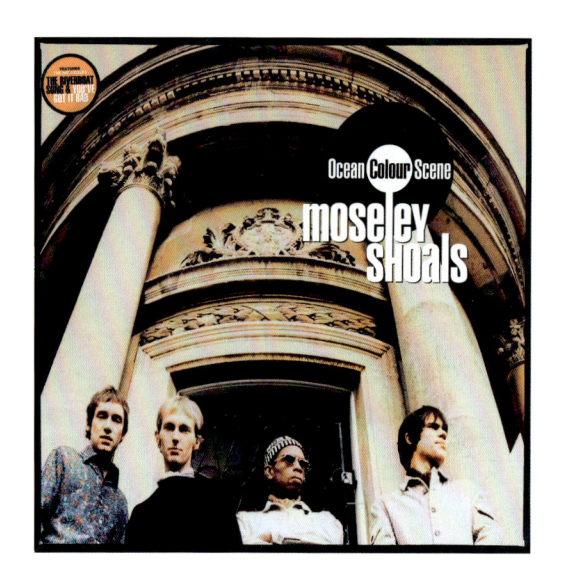

Special mention must also be made of Britpop's leading lights, Oasis, for whom clothes were of great importance. Their initial look was that of the football terrace: cagoules and trainers. Then they were handed mountains of cash, which rushed them through the revolving door at Gucci. Oasis were never a Mod band *per se* but they did avail themselves of its principles, seeking out certain labels, sporting the right names, donning great sunglasses and cutting their hair in an appealing Mod/Beatle style. Not long ago, Liam Gallagher formed his own clothes company, Pretty Green, which – fittingly enough – is now located on Carnaby Street.

*Top:* Album cover of *Moseley Shoals* by Ocean Colour Scene, 1996

*Opposite:* L to R: OCS as was. Steve Cradock, Damon Minchella, Oscar Harrison and Simon Fowler in 2001

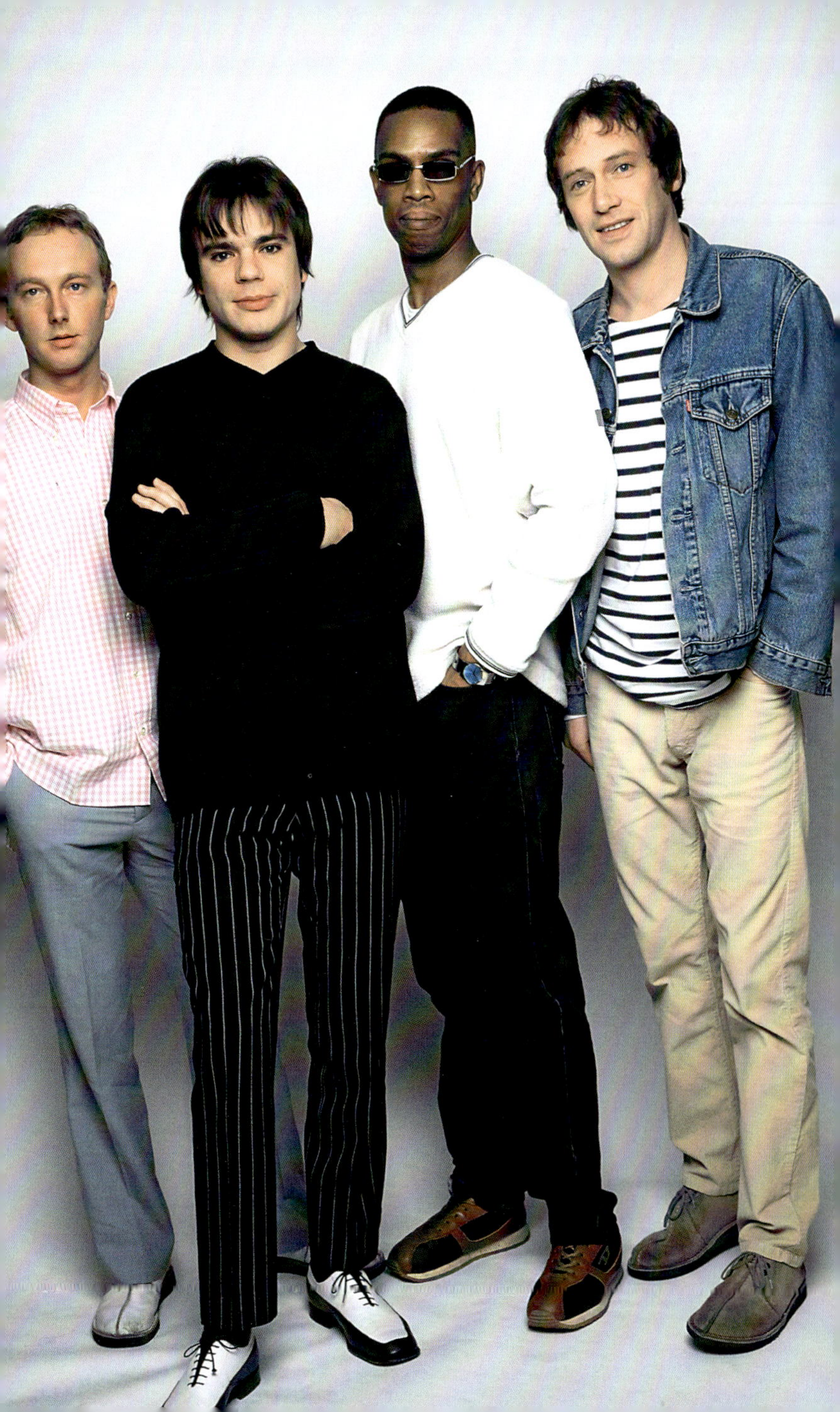

**YOUNG MEN'S SHOES:** Wing-tipped shoe in tan Scottish grain (leather or rubber sole) hand-lasted in England. The domestic shoe is made of smoked elkhide (washable with soap and water) with a tan leather saddle. Brooks' celebrated brown buckskin shoe (crêpe rubber sole) is also hand-lasted to our special order in England.

# Brooks Brothers

*Top, bottom and opposite top:* Brooks Brothers clothing through the decades

*Opposite middle:* The Brooks Brothers logo

*Opposite bottom:* The iconic oxford cloth button-down with the essential 'roll' collar, simply a thing of beauty

The Brooks Brothers shirt is a staple of the Mod wardrobe. It features a roll-neck button-down collar, pleats and a top pocket and comes in 100% oxford cotton. It sports a Golden Fleece logo of a sheep held by a piece of ribbon, which was originally a wool merchants' symbol. For discerning Mods, American-made shirts are the only game in town, and a Brooks Brothers number is a must-buy item.

The Brooks Brothers Company invented the button-down shirt. John E. Brooks, grandson of founder Henry Brooks (who started the company in 1818), noted the shirt collars of polo players flying into their faces as they roared around the pitch on their ponies. His solution was the button-down collar, which made him and the company a fortune. Singer-songwriter Kevin Rowland kitted out his band Dexys Midnight Runners in Brooks Brothers clothing for their album *Don't Stand Me Down* (1985), and a current favourite of Mod style-watchers is the US TV series *Mad Men*, for whose principal male actors Brooks Brothers supplies clothes. Brooks Brothers clothes also feature heavily in Graham Marsh and J. P. Gaul's excellent book *The Ivy Look*.

FEDERICO FELLINI
LA DOLCE VITA
DISTRIBUZIONE
CINERIZ
MARCELLO MASTROIANNI · ANITA EKBERG
ANOUK AIMEE · YVONNE FURNEAUX · ALAIN CUNY · ANNIBALE NINCHI
WALTER SANTESSO e MAGALI NOEL · LEX BARKER · JACQUES SERNAS e con NADIA GRAY
UNA CO-PRODUZIONE RIAMA FILM, ROMA
PATHE CONSORTIUM CINEMA, PARIGI
TOTALSCOPE
MARCHIO DEPOSITATO DALL'A.T.C.
REALIZZATA DA GIUSEPPE AMATO

# Cinema

In its infancy Mod borrowed from Britain's small but influential beatnik scene and in doing so it developed an admiration for all things Continental, from the work of Jean-Paul Sartre to the clothes of Marcello Mastroianni. In London a few cinemas, such as the Academy on Oxford Street, ran European films and Mods were often to be found scattered in the audience, looking cool. They looked studious but in reality were checking out the latest male European styles. An important film in this process was *A Bout de Souffle* (1960), a landmark film of the French New Wave. The film was developed from an idea by director François Truffaut and directed by Jean-Luc Godard. It starred Jean-Paul Belmondo and American actress Jean Seberg. The story is quite simple. Michel (Belmondo) is a petty criminal on the run after shooting a policeman. His girlfriend Patricia (Seberg) sells the *New York Herald*

*Opposite:* Film poster for *La Dolce Vita*

*Top:* Jean-Paul Belmondo smokes up a storm as 'Michel' in a still from the film *A Bout de Souffle*

L to R: Maureen Lipman, Suzy Kendall and Adrienne Posta, from the film *Up the Junction*, based on the book by Nell Dunn

*Tribune* on the streets of Paris and unwittingly hides him in her apartment. Upon learning of Michel's crime she betrays him, and he is finally shot and killed in his attempt to escape from the authorities.

Filmed entirely in Paris on hand-held cameras, with the dialogue written on the spot, *A Bout de Souffle* (which translates into English as 'at breath's end' or 'breathless') attracted the Mods thanks to its brave and Modernist cinematic style. Belmondo's eye-catching style, including his bum-freezer jacket with patch pockets, the shirt and ties he sports, the jaunty way he wears his hat and his way of smoking, was also of huge interest. Meanwhile, Jean Seberg's equally striking look in the film rendered her the girl all Mods wanted to date.

Another important film, released that same year, was Fellini's classic and ultra-stylised *La Dolce Vita* (1960), which exposed the Roman fashions of the day and, more importantly, made Marcello Mastroianni a key actor for Mods to watch in terms of clothes and style.

Surprisingly, apart from *Quadrophenia* (see Quadrophenia – The Film), British cinema has never dealt with the Mod scene *per se*. It has certainly made films that have touched upon it – 1967's *Smashing Time*, for example – but has never engaged with Mod in the same manner that Sidney J. Furie did with Rockers in his much-acclaimed 1964 film *The Leather Boys*. Sightings of Mods in cinema are therefore rare, the only real example being Dennis Waterman in a parka and desert boots and on a scooter in the 1968 film

Belmondo and co-star Joan Soborg kiss in a scene from *A Bout de Souffle*

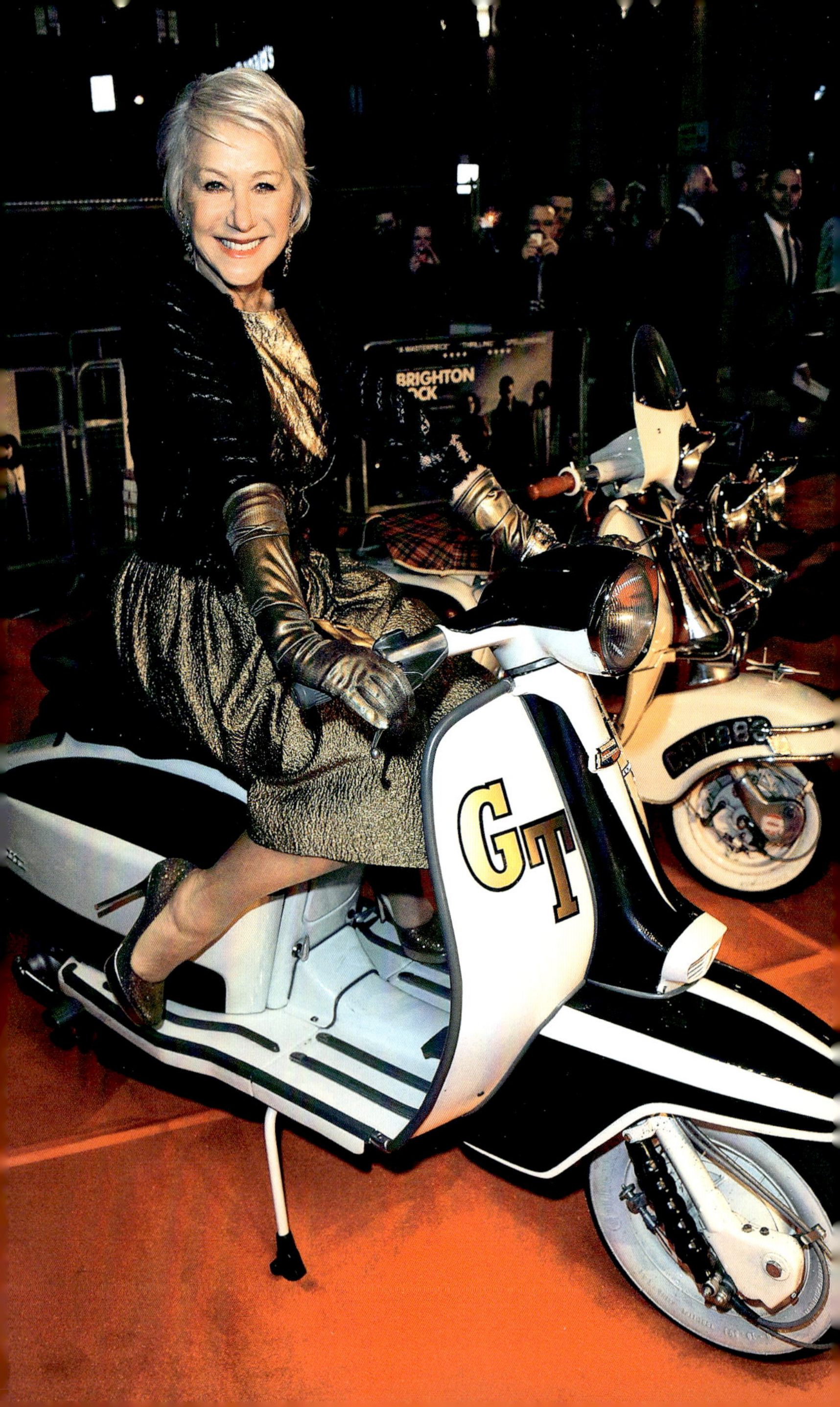
BRIGHTON
GT

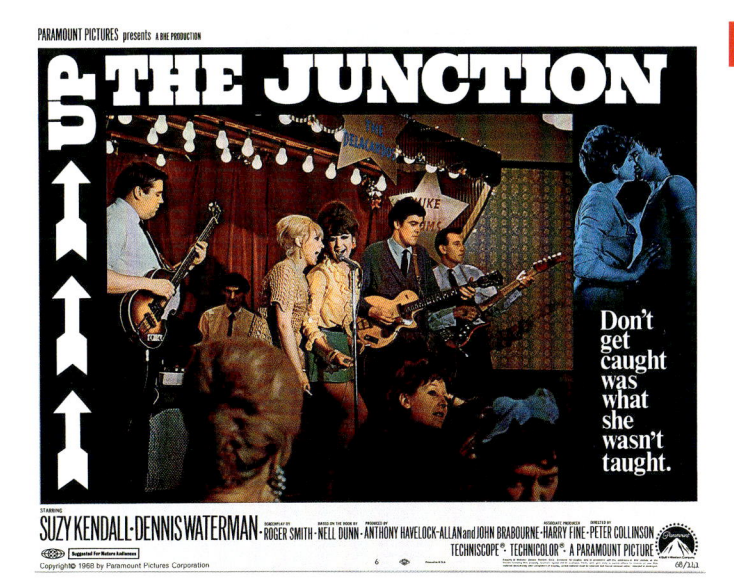

*Up the Junction.* This look was used recently for Rowan Joffe's remake of *Brighton Rock* (2011), which was set in Brighton in 1964. Joffe turns Pinkie, the main character, into a Mod, yet this seems more of an excuse to film parka-clad boys and girls on scooters than an attempt to insert a Mod sensibility into the story.

Some would argue that American films such as *Sweet Smell of Success* (1957), *Mean Streets* (1973) and *Saturday Night Fever* (1977) capture the Mod ethos brilliantly with their stress on clothes and music as an alternative lifestyle. Others argue that the greatest Mod film remains to be made.

*Opposite:* Actress Helen Mirren at the premiere for the film remake of *Brighton Rock*, February 2011

*Top:* The Australian film poster for *Up the Junction*

# Eric Clapton

Sometime in the summer of 1967, graffiti declaring 'Clapton Is God' was sprayed on a wall in North London. That 'Clapton Was a Mod' is more our concern here.

Born in Ripley, Surrey, in 1945, Eric Clapton took to the guitar at the age of 13. His obsession with the instrument was so strong that he was expelled from the Kingston College of Art aged 16 for failing to produce any work. In 1963 he joined The Roosters and then The Yardbirds, where he picked up the nickname 'Slowhand'. He also began immersing himself in black American music and by 1965 was a regular at The Scene Club in Soho, where he would appear dressed head to toe in the Ivy League styles of the day. He bought a lot of his clobber from The Ivy Shop in Richmond. Many remember him as a Face (top Mod) thanks to his immaculate attire. He was probably the first musician to be photographed on stage wearing a Harrington jacket.

*Top:* Pick us a winner, Eric: a Clapton guitar pick

*Opposite:* Eric Clapton performing with The Yardbirds, 1964

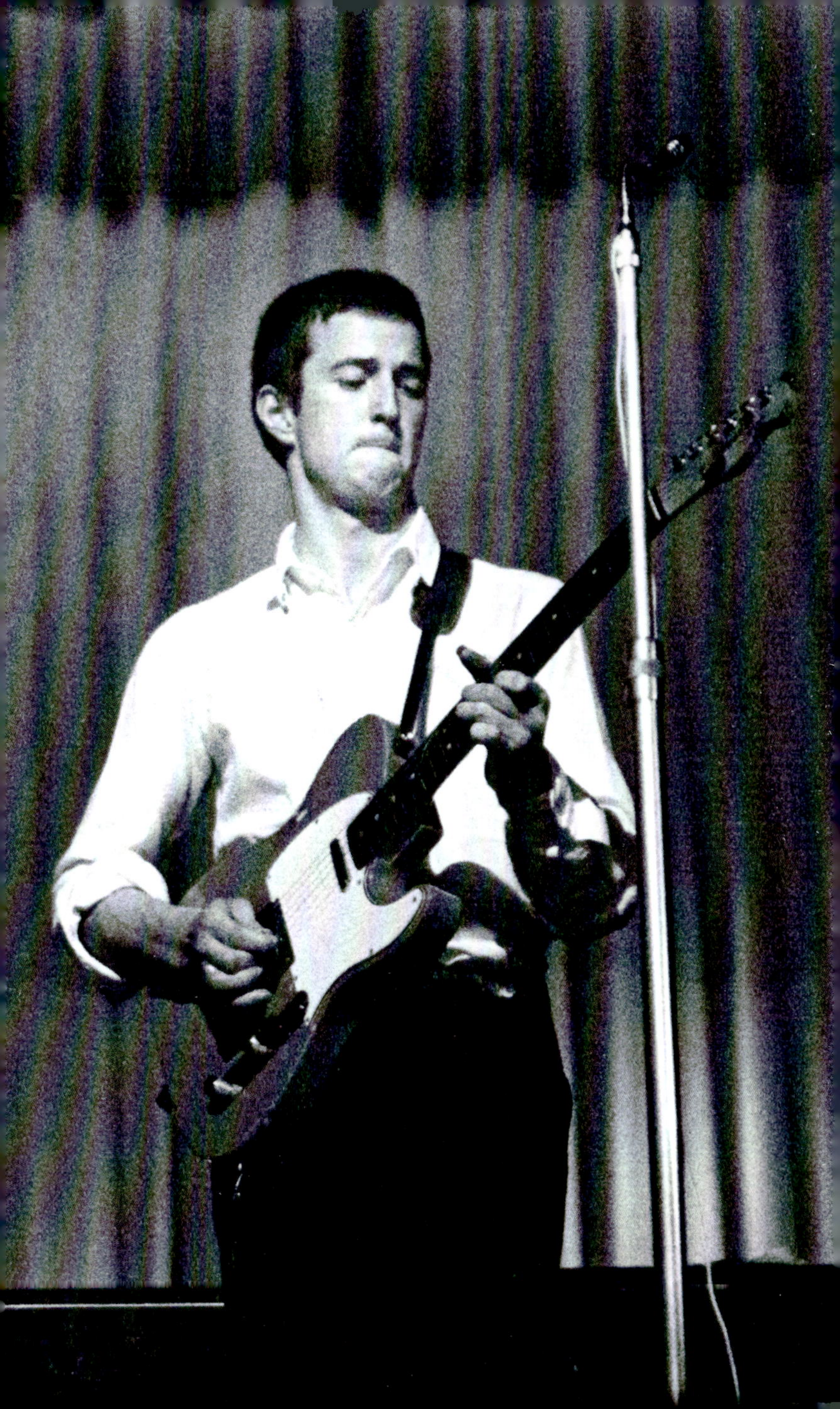

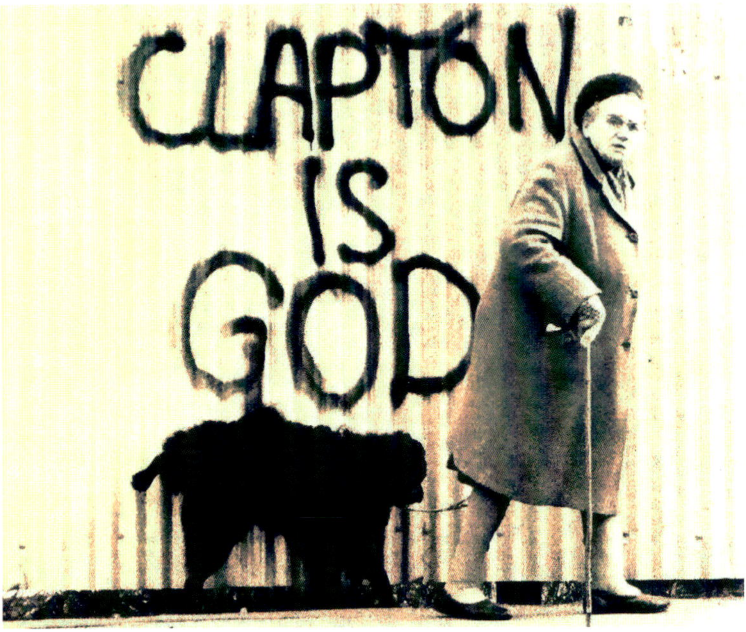
CLAPTON
IS
GOD

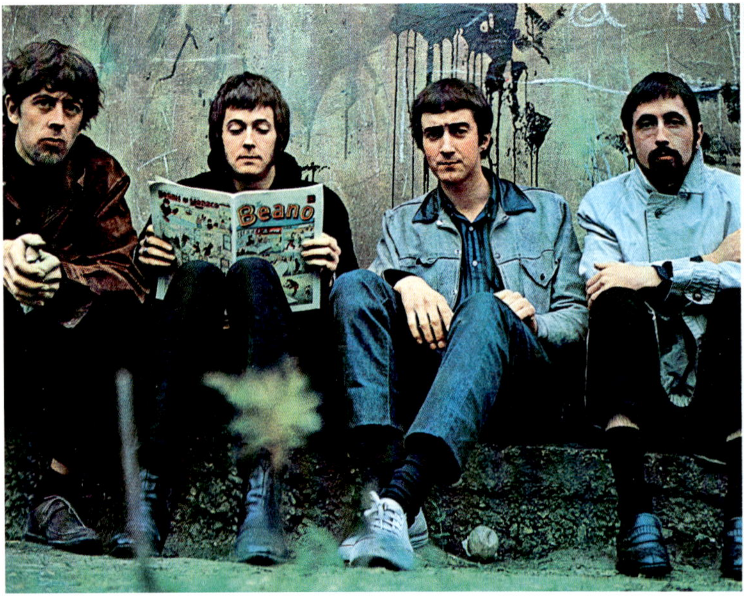
Beano

Clapton went on to find worldwide fame when he teamed up with Ginger Baker and Jack Bruce in the band Cream. He later succumbed to heroin addiction in the early 1970s; this resulted in him founding the Crossroads Centre in Antigua, which offers treatment to alcoholics and drug abusers. Clapton continues to play the blues to sold-out crowds around the world.

*Opposite top:* The dog ain't having it: that famous graffiti

*Opposite bottom:* John Mayall's Bluesbreakers line-up. L to R: John Mayall, Clapton, John McVie and Hughie Flint, 1966

*Top left:* Clapton (in yellow) with the The Yardbirds in 1965

*Top right:* A Gibson ES-335 owned by Clapton

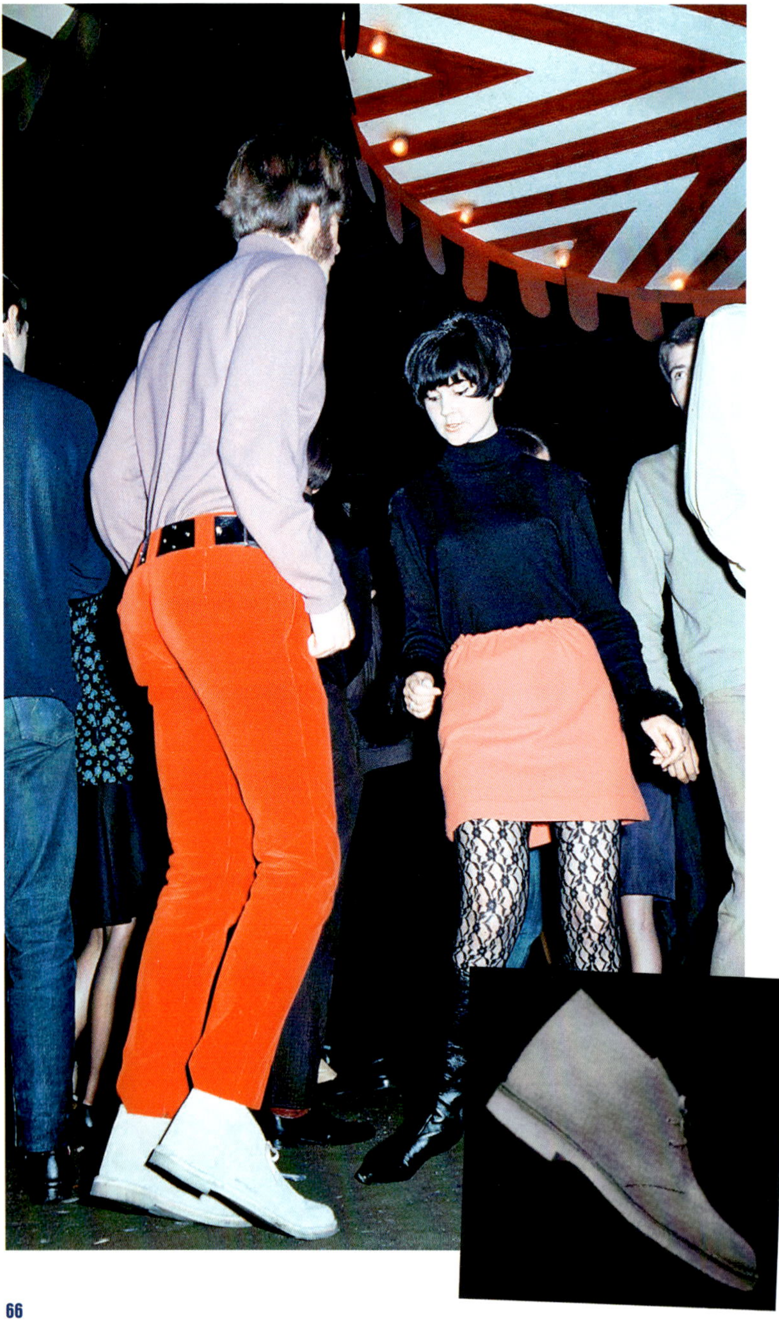

# Clarks Desert Boots

The one item of footwear forever associated with Mods is the Clarks desert boot. That's because it is practical, comfortable and above all highly versatile. A pair can be worn with Levi's jeans or a Mod's pride and joy, the bespoke suit, to equal effect.

The Clarks Shoe Company was started by two Quaker brothers, James and Cyrus Clark, in 1825. The desert boot itself was designed by Nathan Clark in 1949. He based his idea on the footwear worn by off-duty British Army officers in Egypt during the Second World War. The shoe went straight into production and the company has never looked back.

The desert boot is instantly recognisable for its crêpe sole and two-eyelet feature and has been a consistent seller. In recent years the company have also introduced the Clarks Originals label, recreating certain styles from its archives. They have also collaborated with

*Opposite main:* A young Mod on the two-step sporting a fine pair of classic Clarks desert boots, 1967

*Opposite inset:* The two-eyelet suede beauty!

*Top:* Advertisement for Clarks shoes, 1944

the likes of Pretty Green, the clothing company fronted by ex-Oasis frontman Liam Gallagher, on limited editions. Like the desert itself, this shoe endures.

*Top:* The Clarks factory in full swing, *circa* 1920s

*Opposite top:* 'Originals' creator James Clark

*Opposite bottom left:* Modern-day advert for the desert boot

*Opposite bottom right:* Illustration showing the Clarks factory in Street, Somerset

Clarks days
are back again.

C&J.CLARK STREET, Somersetshire.

MANUFACTURERS OF
Ladies, Gentlemens & Childrens BOOTS, SHOES & SLIPPERS. Fair Wear Guaranteed.

JEFF KRUGERS
JAZZ AT THE
Flamingo
ere is the internationally famous
FLAMINGO
DRINK
Coca-Cola
CLUB
DOWNSTAIRS
N TONIGHT
Attractions
ES PREMIER
YTHM-BLUES-CLUBS
OPEN
NIGHT
WANTED
URGENTLY
TOP MACHINISTS
TOP PRESSER
OVERLOCKING-MACHINE
TOP WAGES PAID
SIMON'S FASHIONS

# Clubs Past

Clubs have always played a crucial role in developing youth cultures. They are where new fashions are sported and new music is adopted. One of the very first of the important Mod clubs was called The Flamingo and was opened in 1952 by the impresario Jeffrey Kruger. Kruger worked for a film company and was a huge jazz fan. Yet every jazz venue he visited was dowdy and downmarket. He envisioned jazz being played in a much smarter environment to an equally smart crowd. To achieve this end, Kruger started running a jazz club in the basement of The Mapleton Hotel, situated near London's Leicester Square. Not long after, due to heavy demand, he switched location to a club on nearby Wardour Street and named it The Flamingo after one of his favourite jazz songs. The club occupied a small basement and although the capacity was said to be 400, close to 600 people would often

*Opposite:* The entrance to The Flamingo Club, 1966

Mr Jeffrey Kruger relaxes with his canine friends

cram in to hear artists of the calibre of Billie Holiday and Dizzy Gillespie.

Jazz, however, was overtaken by the arrival of rock'n'roll and then rhythm and blues, music that made its impact with short, sweet shocks. As its popularity faded, rhythm and blues music came to the fore and a different crowd began to appear in the club. Kruger's audience was now primarily made up of black American servicemen, Caribbeans and Mods. The music policy at 'The Mingo' reflected this change: music by the likes of Jimmy Smith, James Brown and Prince Buster was played by DJs such as Count Suckle. In terms of live performances, the star of the Saturday all-nighters was Georgie Fame and his Blue Flames, and the excitement that they created at the club is perfectly captured on their album *Rhythm and Blues at The Flamingo*, released in 1964. Other performers, such as Chris Farlowe and Zoot Money, were popular too.

All clubs live on borrowed time. The Flamingo went through a few name changes in an attempt to keep up with the times but within a few years it had gone. Yet its name remains forever enshrined in Mod history.

For anyone interested in Mod culture, a trip to Ham Yard in Soho is essential. This is where The Scene Club, a legendary Mod club of the early 1960s, once stood. The club's address itself derives from The Ham public house, which had stood there as far back as 1739. Today the pub has gone and as for the yard, there is not much to see, except a patch of concrete and bricks.

Young Mods strike a pose on their scooters outside The Scene Club in 1964

Interior of The Flamingo Club, May 1964

But back in 1963 it was the place to go. The club was situated in a basement at 41 Great Windmill Street, opposite The Windmill Theatre. The space had previously been home to jazz clubs in the 1920s and skiffle clubs in the 1950s. The club's main DJ was Guy Stevens, a very influential figure who was later hired to run Sue Records by Chris Blackwell. Stevens's collection of rare and imported records made him one of the leading DJs in London. As well as Stevens on the decks, live acts would occasionally play. Club membership cost a guinea (one pound and five pence), with the Saturday all-nighters costing five shillings. The interior of The Scene was very basic, with padded walls and cushions scattered on the floor. Only soft drinks were sold at the bar, although drug raids by the police were a common occurrence. The club's soundtrack was made up of James Brown, Muddy Waters, The Impressions, John Lee Hooker, Prince Buster

Long after tonight is all over: a young couple exhausted after an all-nighter in Soho

Outside Tiles, 1967

and Jimmy McGriff, among others. Many import records also got their first airing in the UK at The Scene. Its regulars included Eric Clapton and Pete Meaden, who would later manage The Who.

Guy Stevens went on to produce Mott the Hoople and The Clash. He died aged just 38 in August 1978 after years of drink and drug problems. In late 2009 a club night started called 'Ham Yard' in honour of the original club and its music. Smart dress is essential for entry.

Located at 100 West End Lane, NW6, The Railway Hotel was the home of another great Mod club, Klooks Kleek. Situated on the first floor, it was opened on 11 January 1961 by Dick Jordan, primarily as a venue for jazz. Mystery surrounds the origin of the name, but it is thought to be named after an obscure jazz album. Noting the upsurge of interest in young white guys playing American rhythm and blues music, Jordan began to run a regular r'n'b night on Tuesdays. The room itself was tiny, 20 metres square. It was carpeted and heavy red flock wallpaper adorned the walls. It had no stage, lighting or sound engineers. Gigs there were often described as being like seeing someone play in your own front room, yet the list of the club's performers is highly impressive: The Who, The Yardbirds, The Rolling Stones, T-Bone Walker, Howlin' Wolf, Georgie Fame, Geno Washington, Cliff Bennett, Herbie Goins, Chris Farlowe, Rod Stewart and Graham Bond, among others, played for a die-hard Mod crowd. Next door to The Railway Hotel were the Decca studios where The Beatles had famously failed their audition. It was from there that engineers were persuaded to run cabling from one building to the other, which resulted in live albums by Zoot Money and John Mayall being recorded.

Klooks Kleek ended in December 1970 and was re-named The Moonlight. Many top artists have played this venue, including Pete

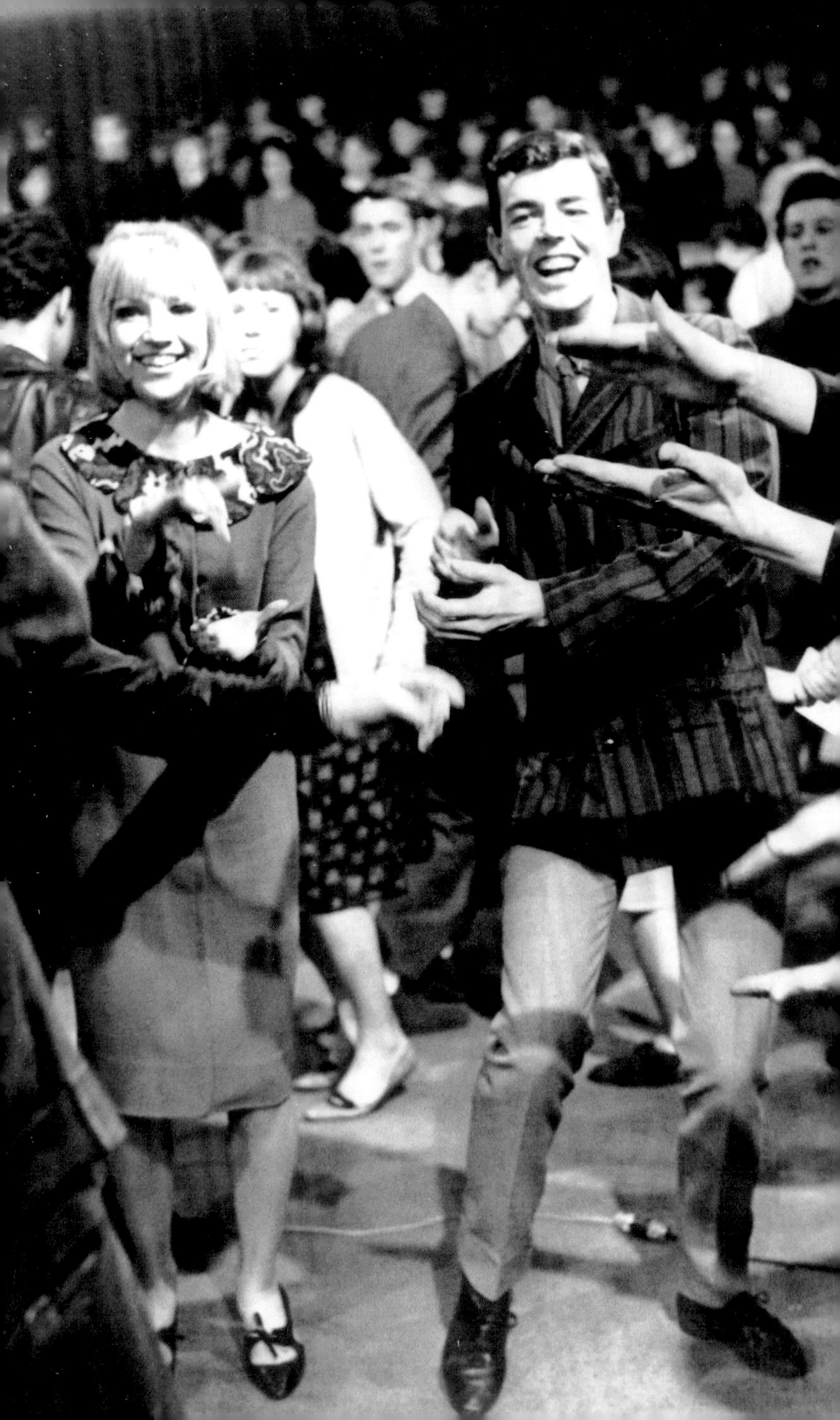

Townshend and The Jam in their early days. The club also held regular Northern Soul nights. The venue, now named The Railway Tavern, is still going strong, with live music most weekends.

Another club of note is Tiles, which was located halfway down Oxford Street. This venue held lunchtime sessions to which young office boys and girls would flock from midday onwards. It was here that the famous author Tom Wolfe came to research his memorable piece on the Mod movement which he named the 'Noonday Underground', a title later picked up by producer and writer Simon Dine for his own band.

*Opposite: Ready, Steady, Go!* dancer Patrick Kerr cuts a rug in The Scene, 1964

*Main:* A stylish crowd gathered for the first night at The Hideaway Club, February 1999

*Inset:* The last ever flyer for The Hideaway, March 2011

# Clubs Present

Three clubs in recent history dominate the current Mod scene: Blow Up, The Hideaway Club and the New Untouchables. First, Blow Up. As a response to the grunge scene of the early 1990s, DJ and club promoter Paul Tunkin hired the upstairs room of the Laurel Tree pub in Camden and started Blow Up, named after the classic 1967 Antonioni film. By using Mod imagery on his flyers, and playing British 1960s rhythm and blues music, classic 1960s TV themes and danceable jazz, Tunkin soon began attracting a sizeable Mod crowd through his door. Increased demand forced Tunkin to take an extra floor in the pub while bringing in Ian Jackson, Andy Lewis and The Karminsky Experience to help out on DJ duties. The short-lived, much-hyped 1994 band Menswear formed at the club.

In 1995 Tunkin started up Blow Up Records; The Weekenders' 'All Grown Up' was his first release. Blow Up then moved to the larger Wag

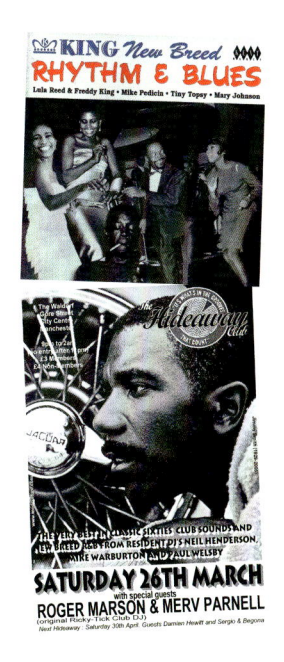

*Top:* CD cover of *King - New Breed Rhythm and Blues*, compiled by The Hideaway Club's DJs

*Bottom:* A Hideaway flyer, March 2005

*Top main:* Twin sisters Paula and Karen, regulars at New Untouchables events

*Top inset and opposite bottom:* Logos for the New Untouchables and their events

Club in 1996. In 2001 it moved again to The Metro Club, located at 4 Denmark Street, the same building that had once housed Regent Sound Studios, where The Beatles, The Rolling Stones and The Kinks had all recorded. Blow Up remains one of London's leading Mod clubs.

Considered a 'club to rival that of The Scene from the 1960s' by original Scene-goers, The Hideaway Club was started in Manchester in early 1999 by Paul Welsby, Neil Henderson and Mike Warburton. Focusing on dance-friendly

Mod sounds, the club soon began attracting a loyal following made up of Northern Soulers, 1950s music enthusiasts and a substantial number of Mods. Such was its popularity, created in part by the founders' musical knowledge, that the Kent Records label (see Kent Records) released two *New Breed* compilations, put together by the boys in 2001 and 2002. In March 2011 it was decided that after 133 nights in three venues – The Waldorf, The Mitre and The Deansgate – it was time to call it a day. Unlike many others, The Hideaway Club went out at the top of its game: in other words, in true Mod style.

Influenced by his parents' Tamla and 1960s pop record collection, the music of The Jam and local heroes The Prisoners, a young Rob Bailey began to attend Mod events in the mid- to late 1980s. Not long after, Rob started to DJ and decided to enter club promotion himself. With a group of friends he started The Untouchables in

*Top left:* Cover of the *New Breed R&B* compilation on the Kent Records label, compiled by The Hideaway's crew

*Top right:* Japanese club flyer for a Blow Up event in 2011

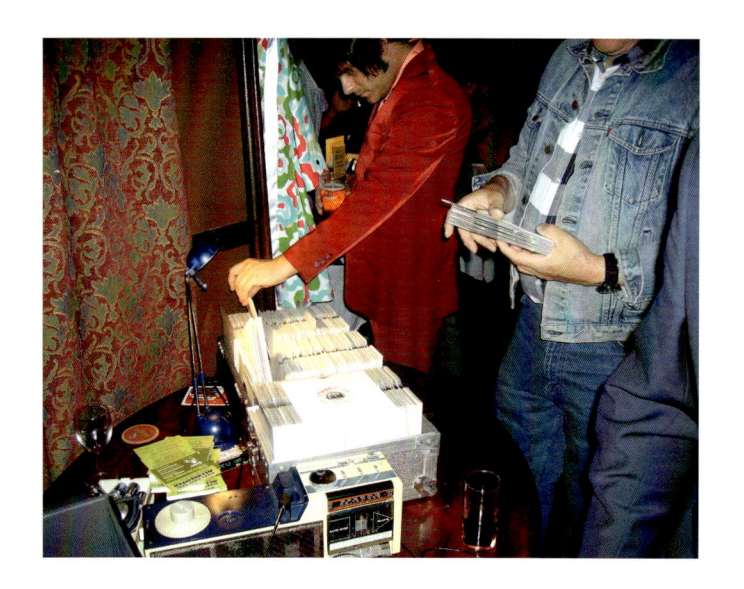

The all-important record stall, this time at The Hideaway Club

1990. They began to produce events and newsletters over the next few years, building a strong following. Rob committed himself to running the clubs and events full-time, setting up the New Untouchables in 1997 with the aim of having a more welcoming approach to various aspects of the scene. With the advent of Britpop in the mid-1990s, a new generation of kids were keen to investigate the music that had influenced the genre. The NUT's operation was the perfect place to show them the way forward.

Today the New Untouchables, assisted by brand manager Pip Pip, are the number one Mod organisation in the world, running regular club nights, including the legendary Mousetrap all-nighters (which celebrated 20 years in 2011), the annual Le Beat Bespoke festival in London every Easter, the Brighton Mod weekender and Euro Ye Ye in Spain, together with Trouble & Tea. Artists they have worked with over the years include The

Sonics, the Stax revue featuring Steve Cropper, Duck Dunn, Eddie Floyd, The Action, Brian Auger, The Pretty Things, Arthur Lee and Johnny Echols of Love, The Undertones, Buzzcocks, Maxine Brown, Flirtations, P. P. Arnold, The Prisoners, The Yardbirds and many more. A bestselling photographic book capturing this scene by Horst A. Friedrichs, titled *I'm One: 21st Century Mods*, was published in 2009.

Hideaway Club founders, promoters and DJs. L to R: Paul Welsby, Mike Warburton, Neil Henderson, July 2000

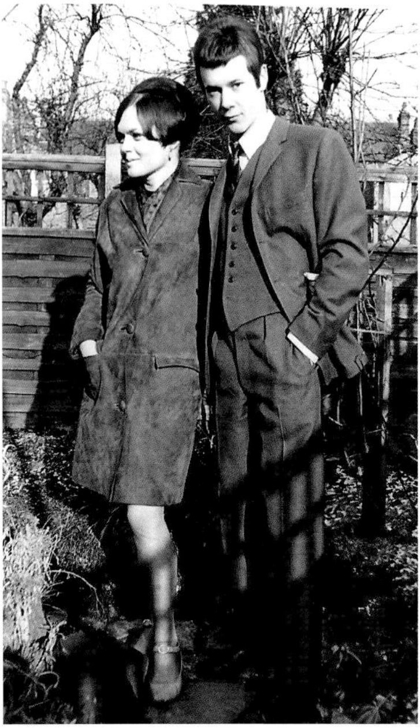

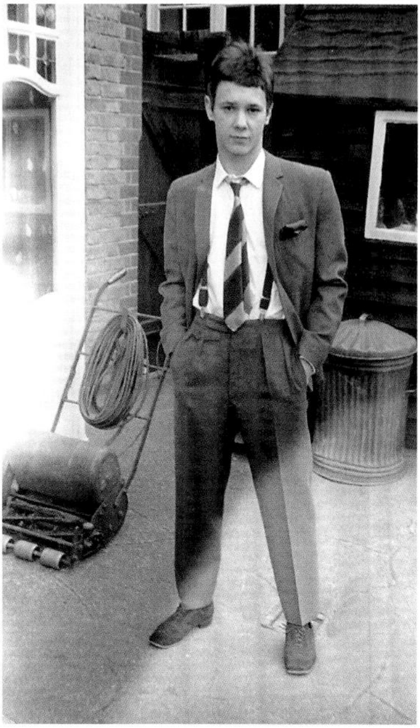

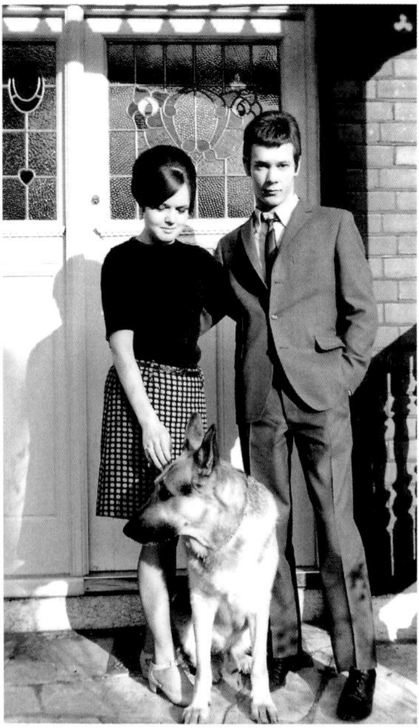

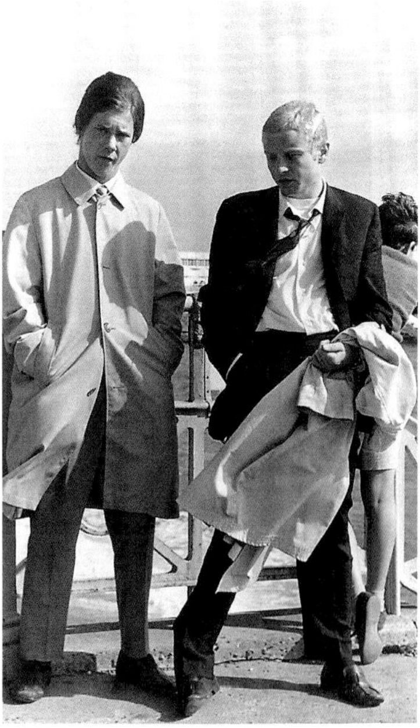

# Randy Cozens

Not all great Mods acquire vast fame. Randy Cozens was an original 1960s Mod who dedicated his life to spreading the gospel about soul music. His enthusiasm was such that it led him to start the famous 6Ts club with Ady Croasdell. He also influenced numerous DJs, writers and soul-scene regulars through his legendary tapes and habit of giving away rare singles to those he considered worthy. Cozens's rugged determination to give soul music the media spotlight it deserved was displayed when in the late 1970s he wrote letter after letter to music papers such as the *NME* and *Sounds*, urging young Mods to explore their heritage of great soul music. Such was his persistence that *Sounds* finally asked Cozens to produce a top 100 soul chart. This chart is now legendary. It not only drew together some of the greatest records ever released but served to influence a generation, putting the likes of Eddie Piller onto

*Opposite top and bottom left:* Randy with his wife, Dawn

*Opposite top right:* Even when gardening, Randy had to look his best

*Opposite bottom right:* Randy and pal at the seaside

*Top:* Randy Cozens in sheepskin

a musical journey which would literally change and colour their whole lives. When it came to music, Cozens had no truck with musical elitism or club politics.

Many recall how if they could not locate a record Randy had recommended he would simply give them his own copy. Tragically, Cozens died of cancer in June 2003, but even as the end approached, he could be found discussing for hours a Maxine Brown (his fave girl singer) single or a great B-side. He was an obsessive maker of tapes and these would serve to spread the word among the soul community. Like all great Mods, he leaves behind a legacy that shines on.

*Left:* Randy and friend sport waistcoats

*Right:* Randy in the late 1970s

Page 18  **BLACK ECHOES**  June 17, 1978

# Old mods never die!

*WHILE Northern Soul music will never date and the dancing is out on its own, the clothes are relics that should be replaced.*

This and only this will send the scene to the bottom of the whirlpool. I think fashion has a lot to do with why a lot of people have crossed over to Disco / Funk. When a gap occurs attract new faces to fill the hole;

There would be no need to dress up like a punk [that's just about as dated anyway] and I'm a bit of a relic myself, at 29 perhaps I shouldn't be allowed to all-nighters [just ask my wife!], but I like to think of myself as at least a little bit modern in the way I dress.

On the London all-nighter scene of the early and mid Sixties fashion changed what seemed like every fortnight and although my music tastes have not changed— I'm a Soul fan and not just what is now known as Northern — I am still, at this ripe ole' age, fashion conscious. Old mods never die they just change their clothes.

And out with the clothes **must go** the likes of Sandie Shaw, Helen Shapiro, Jackie Trent, etc. Enough said! Please don't write about them in your column Rambler.

More importantly can you let people know about an event that takes place in London once a month. Sixties Soul is the name of the game, the emphasis is on dancers but what makes it such a unique event is that the occasional slow classic is mixed in.

It's the same formula that made the London clubs of the Sixties like The Last Chance, The Scene, The Disc, Tiles and Flamingo etc, so legendary. DJ is Terry Davis, refugee from The Wheatsheaf and Shades.

People are travelling from all over the South, Worthing, Hemel, Kent, Weybridge, etc., just to get to the mid-week venue for three and a half hours of pure magic. And while I'm on the subject they are the friendliest crowd I've ever come across, step on a toe or stub a fag on an arm and you'll still get a smile.

Next date is June 28, presented by OBJ's at 'The Prince of Wales', Dalling Road [off King St.], Hammersmith W6, 7.30 p.m. It is now a regular last Wednesday of every month. It's best to go early as everyone so far has been packed to capacity. Oh yes, admission is 50p [70p after 9 p.m.].

— RANDY COZENS
London, N14

Article written by Randy Cozens for *Black Echoes* magazine, 1978

# Randy's Fam

1. *'Whatcha Gonna Do About It'*
   Doris Troy (Atlantic)
2. *'So Far Away'*
   Hank Jacobs (Sue)
3. *'Come See About Me'*
   Nella Dodds (Pye Int)
4. *'Hole in the Wall'*
   George Stone (Stateside)
5. *'Que Sera Sera'*
   The High Keys (London)
6. *'Getting Mighty Crowded'*
   Betty Everett (Fontana)
7. *'I Don't Wanna Fuss'*
   Sugar Pie De Santo (Pye Int)
8. *'Walking the Dog'*
   Rufus Thomas (London)
9. *'Hold What You Got'*
   Joe Tex (Atlantic)
10. *'Time Is On My Side'*
    Irma Thomas (Liberty)
11. *'I Can't Believe What You Say'*
    Ike and Tina Turner (Sue)
12. *'The Drifter'*
    Ray Pollard (UA)
13. *'Any Day Now'*
    Chuck Jackson (Stateside)
14. *'The Monkey Time'*
    Major Lance (Columbia)
15. *'La De Da, I Love You'*
    Inez and Charlie Foxx (Sue)
16. *'The Cheater'*
    Bob Kuban and the In Men
    (Stateside)
17. *'I'm In Your Hands'*
    Mary Love (King)
18. *'The Jerk'*
    The Larks (Pye Int)
19. *'I Had a Talk With My Man'*
    Mitty Collier (Pye Int)
20. *'Oh No Not My Baby'*
    Maxine Brown (Pye Int)
21. *'Gotta Have Your Love'*
    The Sapphires (HMV)
22. *'Everybody Needs Somebody to Love'*
    Solomon Burke (Atlantic)
23. *'La La La La La'*
    The Blendells (Reprise)
24. *'Ride Your Pony'*
    Lee Dorsey (Stateside)
25. *'Selfish One'*
    Jackie Ross (Pye Int)

# ous Mod 100

26. *'Tired of Being Lonely'*
    The Sharpees (Stateside)
27. *'El Watusi'*
    Ray Barretto (Columbia)
28. *'Treat Her Right'*
    Roy Head (Vocallion)
29. *'Who's Cheating Who?'*
    Little Milton (Chess)
30. *'Out of Sight'*
    James Brown (Philips)
31. *'Mercy Mercy'*
    Don Covay (Atlantic)
32. *'Open the Door to Your Heart'*
    Darrell Banks (Stateside)
33. *'A Little Piece of Leather'*
    Donnie Elbert (Sue)
34. *'Go Now'*
    Bessie Banks (Red Bird)
35. *'Searching for My Love'*
    Bobby Moore (Chess)
36. *'You Can't Sit Down'*
    Phil Upchurch Combo (HMV)
37. *'The Duck'*
    Jackie Lee (Fontana)
38. *'Doctor Love'*
    Bobby Sheen (Capitol)
39. *'She Blew a Good Thing'*
    The American Poets (London)
40. *'Watch Your Step'*
    Bobby Parker (Sue)
41. *'Love Ain't Nothin''*
    Johnny Nash (Pye Int)
42. *'Randy'*
    Earl Jean (Colpix)
43. *'Rancid Polecat'*
    Ian and the Clarks (Liberty)
44. *'Oowee Baby I Love You'*
    Fred Hughes (Fontana)
45. *'A Touch of Venus'*
    Sandy Wynns (Fontana)
46. *'Don't Let Me Be Misunderstood'*
    Nina Simone (Philips)
47. *'Ain't Love Good, Ain't Love Proud'*
    Tony Clark (Pye Int)
48. *'I've Got a Woman'*
    Jimmy McGriff (Sue)
49. *'Candy'*
    The Astors (Atlantic)
50. *'Smokey Joe's La La'*
    Googie Rene Combo (Atlantic)

# Randy's Fam

51. 'Mr Bang Bang Man'
    Little Hank (London)
52. 'It's Rough Out There'
    Jerry Jackson (Cameo)
53. 'Oh How Happy'
    Shades of Blue (Sue)
54. 'Ain't Nobody Home'
    Howard Tate (Verve)
55. 'Dimples'
    John Lee Hooker (Stateside)
56. 'Long After Tonight Is Over'
    Jimmy Radcliffe (Stateside)
57. 'Twine Time'
    Alvin Cash (Stateside)
58. 'Lipstick Traces'
    The O'Jays (Liberty)
59. 'Let the Good Times Roll'
    Bunny Sigler (Cameo Parkway)
60. 'There's Nothing Else to Say Baby'
    The Incredibles (Stateside)
61. 'Peaches and Cream'
    The Ikettes (Stateside)
62. 'What's Wrong With Me Baby'
    The Invitations (Stateside)
63. 'Hole in the Wall'
    The Packers (Pye Int)
64. 'Finders Keepers'
    Gloria Jones (Stateside)
65. 'Nothing Can Stop Me'
    Gene Chandler (Stateside)
66. 'See You at the Go Go'
    Dobie Gray (Pye Int)
67. 'Love Makes the World Go Round'
    Deon Jackson (Atlantic)
68. 'Cool Jerk'
    The Capitols (Atlantic)
69. 'The In Crowd'
    Ramsey Lewis Trio (Chess)
70. 'Rescue Me'
    Fontella Bass (Chess)
71. '60 Minutes of Your Love'
    Homer Banks (Liberty)
72. 'Sweetest Thing This Side of Heaven'
    Chris Bartley (Cameo)
73. 'A Lil' Lovin' Sometimes'
    Alexander Patton (Capitol)
74. 'You've Got to Pay the Price'
    Al Kent (Track)
75. 'Make Me Yours'
    Bettye Swann (CBS)
76. 'The Pain Gets a Little Deeper'
    Darrow Fletcher (London)

## ous Mod 100

77. *'Talk of the Grapevine'*
    Donald Height (London)
78. *'Always Something There to Remind Me'*
    Lou Johnson (London)
79. *'Steal Away'*
    Jimmy Hughes (Pye Int)
80. *'Yes I'm Ready'*
    Barbara Mason (London)
81. *'Gee Whiz'*
    Carla Thomas (Atlantic)
82. *'My Girl Sloopy'*
    The Vibrations (London)
83. *'Gypsy Woman'*
    The Impressions (HMV)
84. *'You Don't Know Like I Know'*
    Sam and Dave (Atlantic)
85. *'I'll Take Good Care of You'*
    Garnett Mimms (UA)
86. *'Nothing Takes the Place of You'*
    Toussaint McCall (Pye Int)
87. *'The 81'*
    Candy and the Kisses (Cameo)
88. *'Mr Pitiful'*
    Otis Redding (Atlantic)
89. *'This Can't Be True'*
    Eddie Holman (Cameo)
90. *'You Got Too Much Going For You'*
    Jimmy Beaumont (London)
91. *'Help Me'*
    The Spellbinders (CBS)
92. *'Higher and Higher'*
    Jackie Wilson (Coral)
93. *'That's Enough'*
    Rosco Robinson (Pye Int)
94. *'I Wanna Be'*
    The Manhattans (Sue)
95. *'Spring'*
    Birdlegs and Pauline (Sue)
96. *'Peace of Mind'*
    The Magnificent Men (Capitol)
97. *'Hey-Sah-Lo-Nay'*
    Mickey Lee Lane (Stateside)
98. *'Mercy'*
    Willie Mitchell (London)
99. *'Gypsy Woman'*
    Derek and Patsy (Island)
100. *'Dr Kitch'*
    Lord Kitchener (Jump Up)

# The Creation

Formed from the embers of British beat group The Mark Four, The Creation hit the recording studios in 1966, with Kenny Pickett on vocals, Eddie Phillips on guitar, John Dalton on bass and Jack Jones on drums. Their first single, produced by Shel Talmy, was called 'Making Time' and was released in June 1966. It reached number 49 in the charts. The follow-up, 'Painter Man', fared a little better, getting to number 36, and going top ten in Germany. Moreover, Phillips displayed his distinctive style on this track by playing his guitar with a violin bow. The band's on-stage style at this point played on the Pop art movement of the time, which, along with their colourful dress sense, explains their attraction for Mods. On stage Pickett would paint a canvas while performing. The painting would then be set on fire. Memorably, Phillips described their music as 'red, with purple flashes'.

Artwork from The Creation's *Singles Collection* compilation

After failing to set the charts alight (!) the band underwent numerous line-up changes, notably with Bob Garner coming in as lead vocalist. Their attempt to break America failed but they remained popular in many parts of Europe. However, in 1967 first Phillips and then Garner left and The Creation folded. A re-formed line-up appeared in the mid-1980s, with Pickett, Phillips and Dalton involved. They were later joined by Garner in 1994. Pickett sadly died in 1997. Phillips continues to tour intermittently. The record label Creation, owned by Alan McGee and home to such neo-Mod bands as Oasis, took its name from the band.

The Creation's first two singles remain big favourites on the Mod club scene and have been used recently in TV adverts. Boney M reached number 10 in the UK charts in 1979 with a cover of 'Painter Man', thus giving some remaining band members some well-deserved royalties.

Purple flash! Bang! Wallop! The Creation take to the stage in Germany in 1966. L to R: Kenny Pickett, Eddie Phillips, Bob Garner

DC Fontana à Paris!

# DC Fontana

Anyone who has recently attended live events featuring bands with a Mod flavour will no doubt have witnessed the incredibly hard-working DC Fontana. The band began in 1993, featuring Mark Mortimer on bass, Nigel Horton on drums, Neil Jones and Lloyd Barnett on guitars and Frazer Douglas on vocals. Over the next few years, by playing a mixture of well-known cover versions and original songs, DC Fontana quickly gained a reputation as a strong live band, appearing at Mod festivals and rallies. Various line-ups have come and gone over the years, but Mortimer has lasted the distance and is very much the guiding light of the band. In 2007 Karla Milton joined after being spotted on MySpace by Mortimer. Working initially as a backing vocalist, Milton was soon handed lead vocalist duties.

Two years ago the band spread their wings, appearing in Italy, France, Greece and Germany.

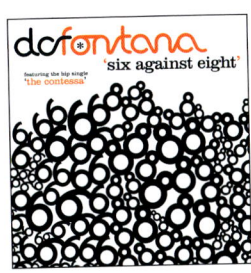

*Top:* Artwork for *La Contessa* CD

*Bottom:* Artwork for *Six Against Eight* release

They also recorded their debut album, *Six Against Eight*, which was released in 2010. An eight-minute promotional film made at Portmeirion, the home of the original *The Prisoner* TV series, and directed by Martin Copland-Gray, soon became an Internet favourite and increased interest in the band. More releases and plenty of live gigs are planned for the future.

*Top:* Karla from the band on stage at Euro Ye Ye, Gijon, Spain, 2010

*Opposite:* DC main man Mark Mortimer

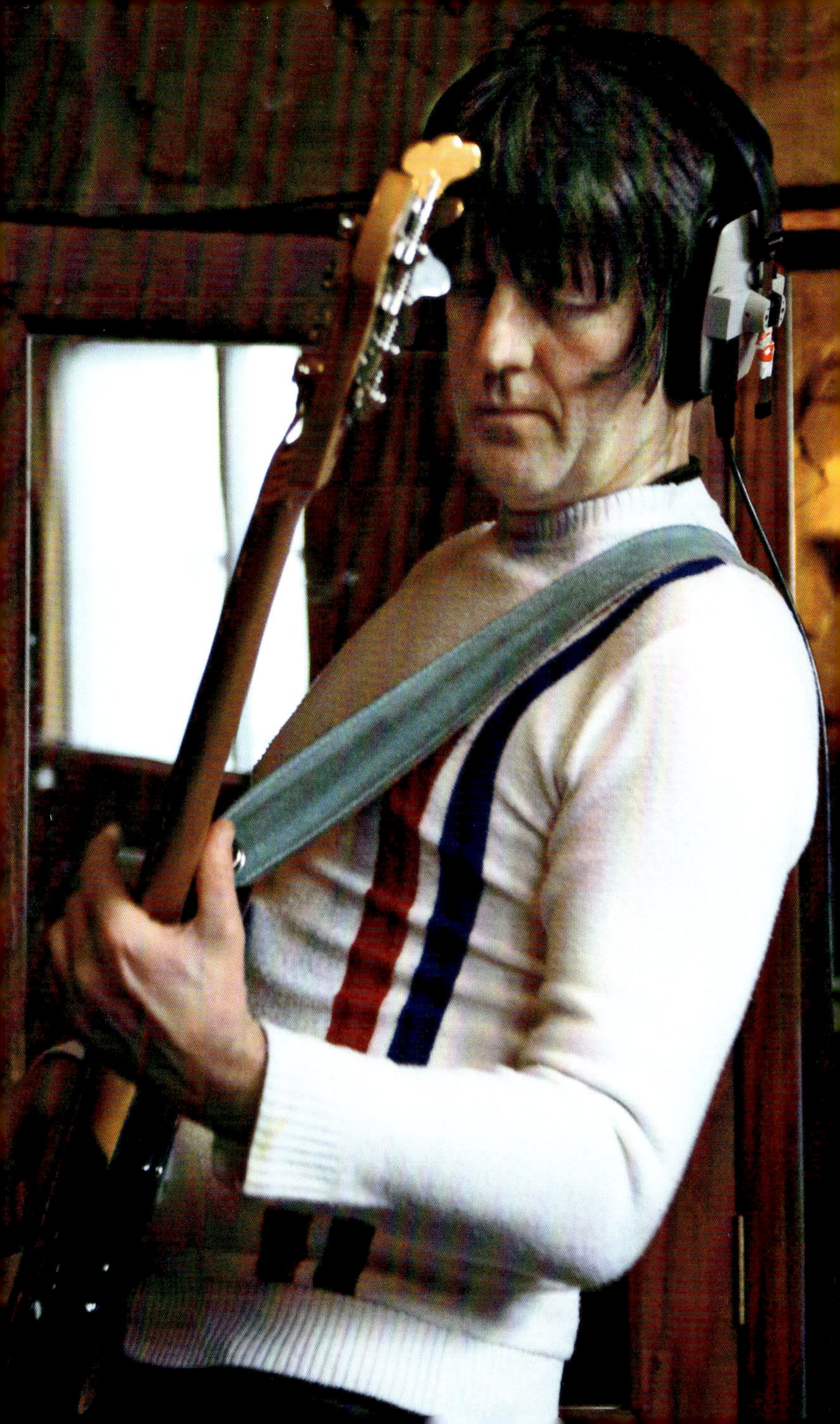

# Julie Driscoll

With her striking eye make-up and elfin haircut, Julie 'Jools' Driscoll created one of the most memorable female Mod looks of the late 1960s. Her unique style was copied by hundreds of girls all over Britain. Born in London in 1947, Driscoll was a singer of note at a very young age. She joined the short-lived band Steampacket in 1965, performing with fellow vocalists Long John Baldry and Rod Stewart as well as Hammond organ aficionado Brian Auger in what is today considered the original supergroup. When the band folded in 1966, Driscoll and Auger teamed up with The Trinity to score a 1968 UK top five hit with the Bob Dylan song 'This Wheel's on Fire'. They also recorded a memorable version of the

Richie Havens song 'Indian Rope Man', which was released as a single in 1969 and remains a favourite at Mod and 1960s clubs to this day. Driscoll married experimental jazz musician Keith Tippett in the early 1970s and they have worked together ever since. She still retains a fab hairstyle.

*Opposite:* Julie in her pomp in early 1969

*Main:* Julie Driscoll on stage at The Marquee Club with Steampacket in 1965

*Inset:* Album cover of *The Best of Julie Driscoll, Brian Augur and The Trinity*, Polydor compilation, 1970

**101**

Poster for an appearance at The Twisted Wheel by Junior Walker and the All-Stars in March 1970

# Roger Eagle

If the South of England had Guy Stevens then the North belonged to Roger Eagle. It was Eagle who manned the decks at The Twisted Wheel in Manchester, one of the UK's most influential clubs. It was here that the foundations of Northern Soul were laid by Eagle. Eagle hailed from a literary family but in the mid-1950s became mesmerised by the sound of early rock'n'roll. By the start of the 1960s he had heard Ray Charles and was a huge rhythm and blues man. In fact, such was his dedication to the music that he began importing American records into the UK, his favoured label being Stax Records. (Eagle was the first man in Britain to play – among many others – 'You Don't Know Like I Know' by Sam and Dave.) In 1963 fate intervened. Eagle was in a Manchester coffee bar examining some tapes he had just received from the USA when two brothers approached him. They were the Abadi brothers and they ran

*Top:* Handbill from The Twisted Wheel, June/July 1969

*Bottom:* Twisted Wheel sew-on patch

L to R: Roger Eagle with blues great John Lee Hooker and Twisted Wheel co-founder Roger Fairhurst

a club called The Twisted Wheel. Would Eagle consider DJing there for £3 a night? Eagle played for seven hours a night and such was the quality and breadth of his set that he was soon drawing soul lovers from all over the country. Eagle also booked great live acts to appear, including Junior Walker, Howlin' Wolf, Sugar Pie De Santo, Georgie Fame and The Spencer Davis Group. When The Rolling Stones visited the club Eagle spotted them and played – track for track – all the original records they had just covered for their debut album. It was a brilliant Mod put-down. However, with the audience swallowing an inordinate amount of pills every night and demanding faster and faster music (thus laying down the roots for the Northern scene), the purist Eagle decided to opt out and start his own operation. 'I had respect for what I was dealing with and I don't think they did', he said of the crowd to *The New Breed* fanzine. In 1966 Eagle went to the Blue Note Club and then started the Stax Club, named after his favourite label. After a couple of years in clubland, Eagle's ear was taken by the progressive rock scene and he set sail for that particular sea. In 1999 he died of cancer, aged just 56. The eagle had flown, but what a legacy he left behind.

*Top:* Roger Eagle (far left) and Roger Fairhurst (2nd right)

*Bottom:* Advertising for The Twisted Wheel

# The Eyes

Formed in Ealing in 1964, The Eyes consisted of Terry Nolder on vocals, Barry Allchin on bass, Phil Heatley and Chris Lovegrove on guitars, and Barry Corcoran on drums. The band's aggressive sound placed them at the centre of the Power Pop art section of Mod music. Despite a succession of fine singles on the Mercury label, chart success eluded them. The band are fondly remembered by aficionados for their song 'I'm Rowed Out', from their rare 1966 EP *The Arrival of the Eyes*, which is still a staple in the Freakbeat section of most contemporary Mod clubs. Their other notable song is 'My Degeneration', a cheeky nod to the classic song 'My

Generation' by The Who. With the commercial failure of their own material, The Eyes began issuing a series of cover versions, including The Beatles' 'Good Day Sunshine'. Their last recorded output was a Rolling Stones tribute album which they released under the name The Pupils. Unfortunately, the band lost their focus and in 1967 they broke up.

*Opposite:* The Eyes – have it!
*Top:* The Eyes in their favoured rugby shirts

# F

Georgie Fame jumps for joy after his single 'Yeh Yeh' knocks The Beatles' 'I Feel Fine' off the top spot on the pop charts, January 1965

# Georgie Fame

One of the leading lights of early Modernism was Clive Powell, who came to prominence as Georgie Fame and became the epitome of the sharp-suited Mod musician. He was born in Lancashire in 1943 and began piano lessons at the age of seven. By his teenage years the young Powell was playing in local bands. At 15 years of age he was discovered at a Butlins Holiday Camp and a year later came to London, where he signed a management deal with the legendary entrepreneur Larry Parnes.

'Mr Parnes, Shillings and Pence', as he was known, had the habit of giving his performers new stage names, and so Clive Powell became Georgie Fame. Soon Georgie was playing with rock'n'rollers such as Eddie Cochrane and Gene Vincent. He soon became dissatisfied with backing duties, and so put together his own band, which he christened The Blue Flames. The band began playing the smaller nightclubs, finally

Album cover of *Georgie Fame – Rhythm and Blues at The Flamingo*. No Mod home should be without a copy…

settling – most famously – at The Flamingo in Soho, where Georgie's sharp dress sense and vast musical repertoire from the worlds of jazz, blue beat and ska made him a natural Mod favourite. He was also much admired by a sizeable number of black American servicemen, who would often bring him import albums by the likes of Mose Allison. Georgie would learn these songs and then perform them the following week, much to their delight.

Success in the pop charts followed when his cover of the Jon Hendricks song 'Yeh Yeh' went to number one in early 1964. His performance of this song on the TV show *Ready, Steady, Go!* is a defining moment in Mod history. Other notable songs include 'Somebody Stole My Thunder' and 'Sitting in the Park'. His biggest chart success came in 1967 with the song 'The Ballad of Bonnie and Clyde'. After working extensively with ex-Animals keyboard player Alan Price in the

'In the Meantime', Georgie Fame and the Blue Flames' single from December 1965

**F**

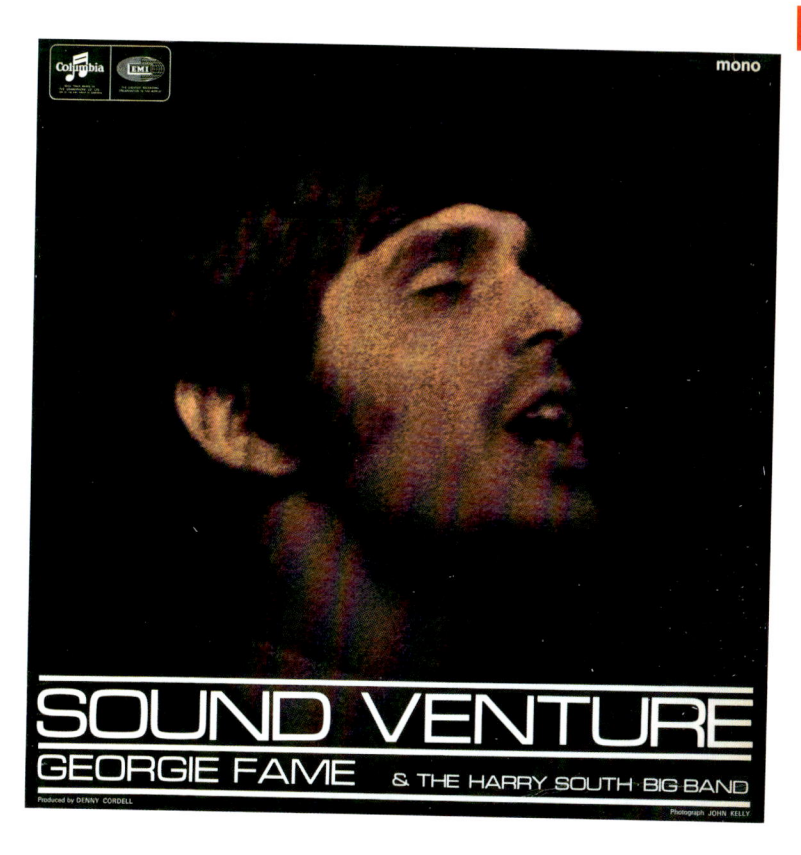

1970s, Fame has collaborated with the likes of Van Morrison and Bill Wyman, while continuing to perform in his own right, often with his sons Tristan and James in his band.

Album cover of *Sound Venture*, recorded with the Harry South Big Band in 1966, which featured many of the UK's top jazz musicians, including Tubby Hayes, Ronnie Scott, Jimmy Deuchar, Phil Seamen and Stan Tracey

*Top and centre:* Issues 13 and 15 of the fanzine *Extraordinary Sensations*, founded by Acid Jazz supremo Eddie Piller

*Bottom:* Issue 8 of *Heavy Soul!*, featuring New Street Adventure. The 'zine is run by Adam Cooper of Rowed Out Records

# Fanzines

One of punk's most enduring legacies was to revive the art of the fanzine. The term 'fanzine' was first coined in 1940 and was used to describe literature produced by fans of a particular genre or cult. In 1976 punk's attack on establishment figures, including the music press, ignited a rush of hastily put-together publications that were then sold at gigs and club nights. In 1979 the Mod revival sparked a similar rush. Three fanzines stood out in particular – *Maximum Speed*, *Extraordinary Sensations* (started by one Eddie Piller) and the lavish *Shadows and Reflections*, edited by Chris Hunt. In some part their enthusiasm helped keep the Mod revival alive.

Today one of the leading Mod fanzines is *Double Breasted*, which first appeared in Scotland during the summer of 2008. Its founders, Jennie and Colin Baillie and Sharon Wood, originally set out to promote and document the Scottish Mod scene. Before long, however, demand for the

A flyer for the 'A Little Mixed Up' event run by the good people behind the *Double Breasted* fanzine, Jennie and Colin Baillie

*Left:* Cover of the *Double Breasted* fanzine

*Right:* Issue 8 of *Heavy Soul!* fanzine

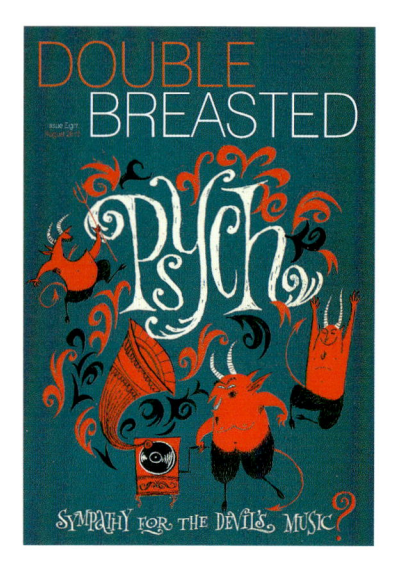

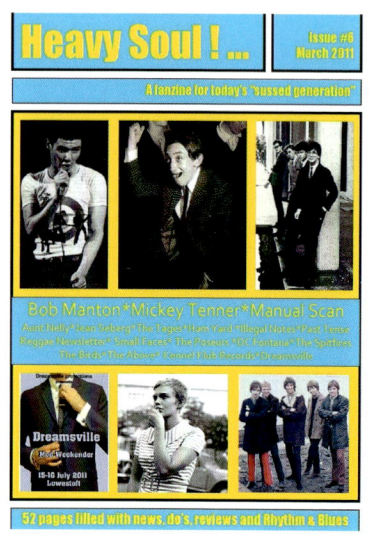

publication started coming from all over the UK. Other countries also got interested; it is not hard to see why. Nicely packaged and full of interesting articles, *Double Breasted* writes engagingly about the scene. Of late, the team have developed the content to include Mod city guides to Rome, Barcelona and New York, as well as focussing on the Mod scene in places such as Mexico. In 2009 the fanzine released a CD of Mod/1960s-influenced bands from Scotland and this in turn led to all-day events in Scotland and London in 2011 featuring the bands chosen. A new CD is due in 2012 and despite the financial constraints of running a fanzine, *Double Breasted* continues to grow at an impressive pace.

The other contender is *Heavy Soul!*, started by Adam at Rowed Out Records. *Heavy Soul!* is

**EXTRAORDINARY SENSATIONS !**
**number fourteen**
OUT IN JANUARY '85

full of enthusiasm which is neatly balanced out by numerous facts pertaining to Mod culture. Carrying strong articles on anything from famous Mods to Brutus shirts, this publication goes from strength to strength.

Does exactly what it says on the tin! Issue 14 of *Extraordinary Sensations*

# Fleur De Lys

Creators of two fine Mod singles, 'Circles' and 'Mud In Your Eye', Fleur De Lys came together in 1964 and hailed from the Southampton area. The band's original line-up consisted of Frank Smith on guitar and vocals, Alex Chamberlain on organ, Danny Churchill on bass and Keith Guster on drums. A year or so into their existence they were discovered by Tony Calder, right-hand man to Andrew Loog Oldham at Immediate Records. 'Moondreams', their debut single, followed in November 1965 and was produced by Jimmy Page. Following the single's release, a succession of line-up changes occurred, which included Gordon Haskell replacing Danny Churchill. In early 1966 the band covered The Who's song 'Circles' so successfully that it is still played today by many Mod DJs. After its release, the band came to the attention of Frank Fenter, head of Atlantic Records in the UK, who was married to the singer Sharon Tandy. Fenter became their

Cover of the 2009 Acid Jazz compilation *The Two Sides of the Fleur De Lys* manager and the band backed Tandy on her classic Freakbeat single 'Hold On'. They also became her live backing band for a while. After their stint with Tandy, the band released the single 'Mud In Your Eye' on the Polydor label. Although chart success eluded them, the song has since assumed Freakbeat classic status.

The band split in 1969. Haskell later had a major chart hit in 2001 with the song 'How Wonderful You Are'. A book, *Circles: The Strange Story of the Fleur De Lys*, written by Paul Anderson and Damian Jones, was released by Acid Jazz Books in September 2009 and the band reformed for a one-off reunion gig at The 100 Club a few months later.

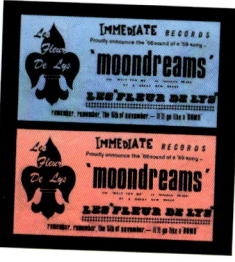

*Top:* Feel the frill: group shot of the band from 1968

*Bottom:* Advert for the band's first single, 'Moondreams', which was released on the Immediate label in November in 1965; they were then known as Les Fleur de Lys

Martin Freeman with a paisley scarf, in a Harrington, with a Union Jack bag: very much the modern Mod

# Martin Freeman

No other actor in living memory has waved the Mod flag quite so enthusiastically as Martin Freeman. Put Mod and Freeman into a search engine and you will discover many an interview in which the actor enthuses about Smedley tops, brogue shoes, seersucker jackets and the Modernist view of the world. Since hitting the big time with projects such as *The Office* and *Sherlock* (for which Freeman won a BAFTA), a lot of his free time and money is spent at tailors such as Soho's legendary Mark Powell, creating new suits and looks to go with his huge record collection. Freeman actually appeared as a Mod in the hit Internet series *Svengali*, and his look and understanding of the whole ethos is clear to see. His style is clean and smart but never overbearing and his love for the genre remains undiminished.

Mr Freeman sports a classic two-button suit, tastefully accessorized, at the London gala premiere of *In the Loop*, 2009

# Galliano

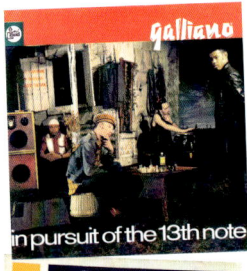

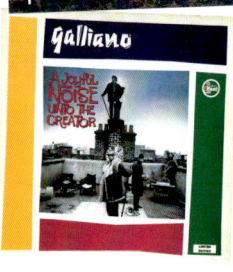

*Top:* Album cover of *In Pursuit of the 13th Note*, released in 1991

*Bottom:* Album cover of *A Joyful Noise Unto the Creator*, released in 1992

Major players in the neo-Mod scene of the early 1990s, Galliano consisted of frontman Rob Gallagher and Constantine Weir on vocals, Michael Snaith on vibe controller and Crispin Robinson on percussion. Signed to the Talkin' Loud record label, Galliano were later joined on vocals by Valerie Etienne. Musicians of the calibre of Mick Talbot (keyboards), Ernie McKone (bass) and Crispin Taylor (drums) complemented the band's live shows. The sound of Galliano was a combination of jazz, soul and funk mixed with a healthy dose of urban street culture. Their natural style centred around the fashion label The Duffer of St George and similar smart street clothing. The mix, then, was British working-class guys taking their cues from hip fashions and black American music. Their debut album of 1991, *In Pursuit of the 13th Note*, was a big favourite for those in the know and songs like 'Stoned Again' and 'Totally Together' still stand

**G**the test of time. Major chart success eluded them until 1994, when their album *The Plot Thickens* reached number seven in the charts. Their single 'Long Time Gone' reached number 15. But it was in a live context that the band proved most potent, remaining extremely popular on the live circuit until their split in the late 1990s. Gallagher continues to record under the name Earl Zinger.

All aboard the good ship Galliano in 1990. L to R: vibe controller Mr Snaith, Rob Gallagher, Constantine Weir

# Glam Rock and Pub Rock

Mod helped build glam rock. An outrageous statement? Consider this. Three of glam rock's major figures were heavily shaped and influenced by Mod in their formative years. Two of them – Marc Bolan and David Bowie – were enthusiastic practitioners of the Modernist life, while the third, Bryan Ferry, discovered the power of the pose through Mod and later aligned it with a deep love of black American music. Mod's great gift to all three was to encourage them to craft a look that would pull them away from the crowd and, in doing so, satisfy their individualistic instincts.

In 1962 Marc Bolan made his first public pronouncement when he was interviewed with his friends Peter Sugar and Michael Simmonds by *Town* magazine. The magazine called them Faces Without Shadows and Bolan filled the article with quotes such as 'You got to be different from the other kids. I mean you got

*Kippington Lodge* EP, with Nick Lowe bottom right

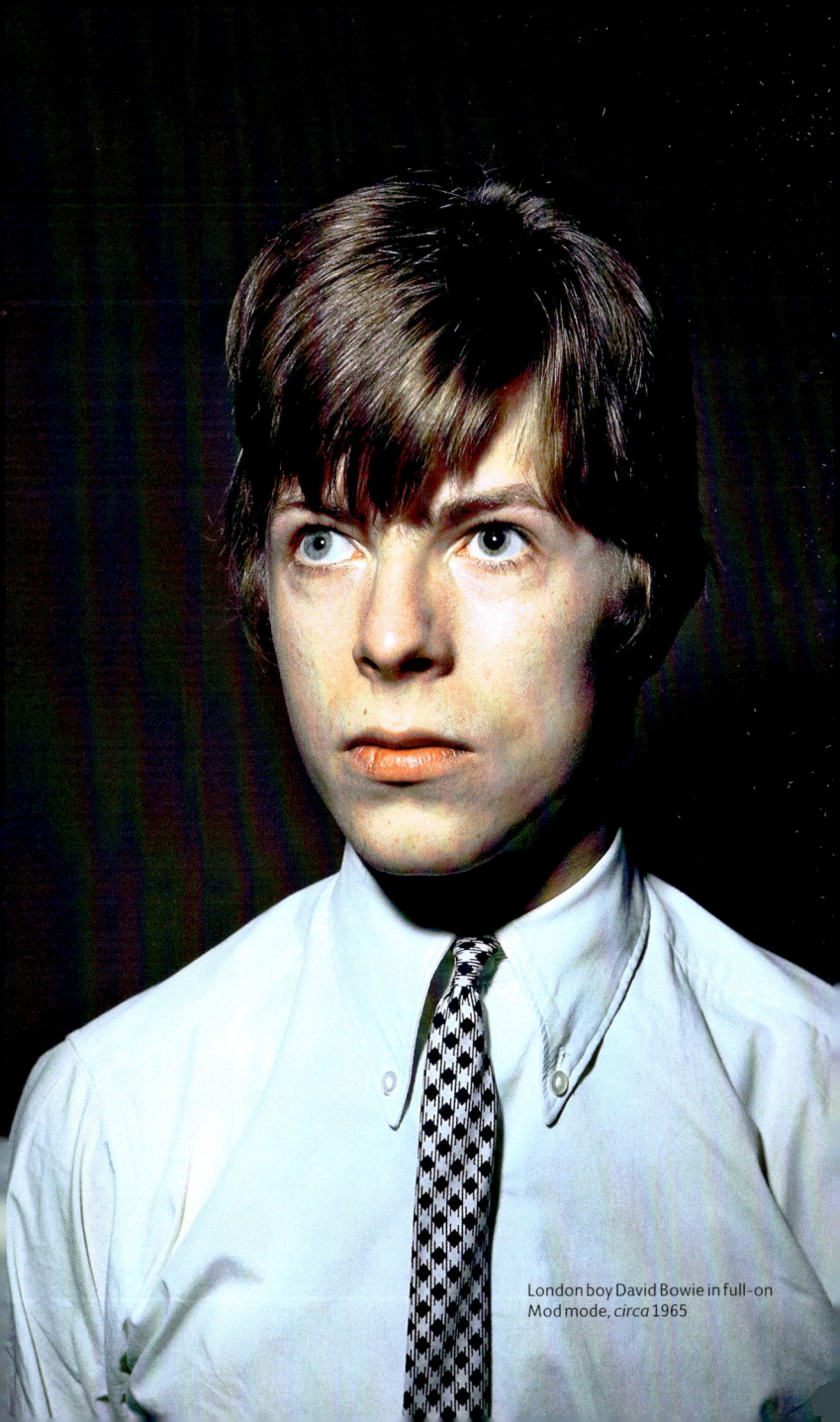

London boy David Bowie in full-on Mod mode, *circa* 1965

to be two steps ahead ... The stuff that half the haddocks you see around wearing ...'. Bolan's Modernism was picked up in North London and translated itself into trips to tailors such as Bilgorri's in Liverpool Street and Leman's in Whitechapel, and onto shoemakers such as Anello & Davide in Covent Garden and Stan Bartholomeu in Battersea. For pleasure there were trips to all the leading Mod clubs, including The Lyceum. One night, Bolan entered that venue with a friend, looked around and said, 'Come on, let's split.' Asked why they were leaving, Marc memorably retorted, 'Too many Mods.' Bolan was always ahead of his contemporaries when it came to clothes and when Mod went national in 1963, you can bet that was the same year he bowed out to explore pastures new.

David Bowie took to Mod in the early 1960s. He had his thick hair cut into a bouffant with a parting at the front and there are stories of

Get it on with Marc Bolan, *circa* 1965

Bowie and his friends travelling to London to pick up discarded clothes from the back of Carnaby Street shops. Bowie was also deeply taken by Mod music – American rhythm and blues – and in many of his early bands, such as The Mannish Boys and Davy Jones and the Lower Third, his repertoire was taken from this deep well of music. Subsequent songs of his, such as 'The London Boys', drew on his Mod experiences. Mod was the trampoline Bowie would use to experiment with many differing styles and it is probably worth asking if his penchant for make-up was first instigated during his Mod days.

Bryan Ferry was raised in Newcastle and as a teenager worked in a clothes shop. It was there that local Mods – and Teddy boys and local stylists – would hang out and the young Ferry would be taught about three-button jackets and the importance of the side vent. Mod fascinated Ferry, for it taught him how to use clothes to draw attention to oneself and to move in a highly stylised manner. His early musical tastes also chimed with the Modernist viewpoint of the world: he loved MJQ and Chet Baker, Charlie Parker and Miles Davis. He was also heavily influenced by American rhythm and blues records, visiting local soul clubs to dance the night away to Tamla, Stax and many others. Although never able to commit himself to one youth cult – apart from the cult of Ferry – Mod undoubtedly played a crucial part in Ferry's development and artistic career.

Jesse Hector was a 1960s Mod who went on to front the 1970s band The Hammersmith Gorillas. Hector's idea for the band was to join glam with Mod and to that end he sported a Mod-ish haircut, button-down shirts and braces with flared trousers. His shot at fame fizzled out, but Hector was one of the handful of Mods that tried to keep the spirit alive during the 1970s.

Another musician with true Mod intent is Nick Lowe. Raised in Modernism as a teenager, Lowe went on to play in the British psychedelic band Kippington Lodge. He later joined the band Brinsley Schwarz, where he would often take to the stage in an eye-catching button-down shirt and a Bowie/Suedeheady haircut. Today Lowe pursues a highly successful solo career, writing songs that bring together the wisdom of soul tinged with the sadness and ironic humour of country music. His is an object lesson in the art of growing old Modfully.

Jesse Hector had his own particular take on it all. Here he is in 1970

# BLUES & SOUL
## MUSIC REVIEW

No. 54  March 5—18, 1971

12½

## WELCOME TO JAMES BROWN

**IKE & TINA TURNER**

**AL GREEN**

**CHUCK BERRY**

**BO DIDDLEY**

PHOTO: JAMES BROWN

# Dave Godin

Dave Godin's achievements within the Modernist world are considerable. He coined the term Northern Soul, ran the UK Motown fan club in the 1960s, created the incredible *Deep Soul* series for Ace Records, produced passionate, highly intelligent and always detailed articles on black music, and was one of the country's leading authorities on African-American music. He was also a keen film buff, a vegetarian and a socialist who in his will left money to a donkey sanctuary. In other words, he was an extraordinary guy.

Born in 1936 in Peckham, London, wartime bomb damage led the Godin family to the leafier area of Bexleyheath in Kent. Dave soon won a scholarship to Dartford Grammar School. It was after hearing the Ruth Brown track 'Mama He Treats Your Daughter Mean' in an ice-cream parlour one day that Godin became hooked on the sounds of rhythm and blues music. Among his peers at school was a young Mick Jagger,

*Opposite:* Copy of a *Blues and Soul* magazine from March 1971. Dave Godin regularly wrote for the mag

Godin (left) with Motown employees, 1965

who soaked up the sounds Godin exposed him to. (They later fell out at the *Ready, Steady, Go!* studios over The Stones's tepid version of Marvin Gaye's 'Can I Get a Witness'.)

During the early 1960s Godin founded the Tamla Motown Appreciation Society and was later recruited by label founder Berry Gordy to be Motown's UK representative. Godin was subsequently responsible for bringing over the 'Motortown Revue of 1965', which starred Smokey Robinson and the Miracles, Martha and the Vandellas and The Supremes. Along with producing the fan club monthly and writing for *Blues and Soul* magazine, Godin also opened Soul City, a record shop and label dedicated to black music. He later scored a number one with the song 'Nothing Can Stop Me' by Gene Chandler. It was while working at Soul City that Godin came up with the phrase 'Northern Soul': a response, he said, to the many requests made in his shop by visiting Northern football supporters for records with a particular sound. Godin's writings on soul music established him as a real authority on the subject and before he died aged 68 in 2004 he compiled the highly acclaimed and essential CD series *Dave Godin's Deep Soul Treasures* for Ace Records. Plans for a major exhibition of his work are currently in negotiation.

The cover of volume 1 of Dave Godin's *Deep Soul Treasures* compilation. This, plus volumes 2, 3 and 4, are essential for any CD collection

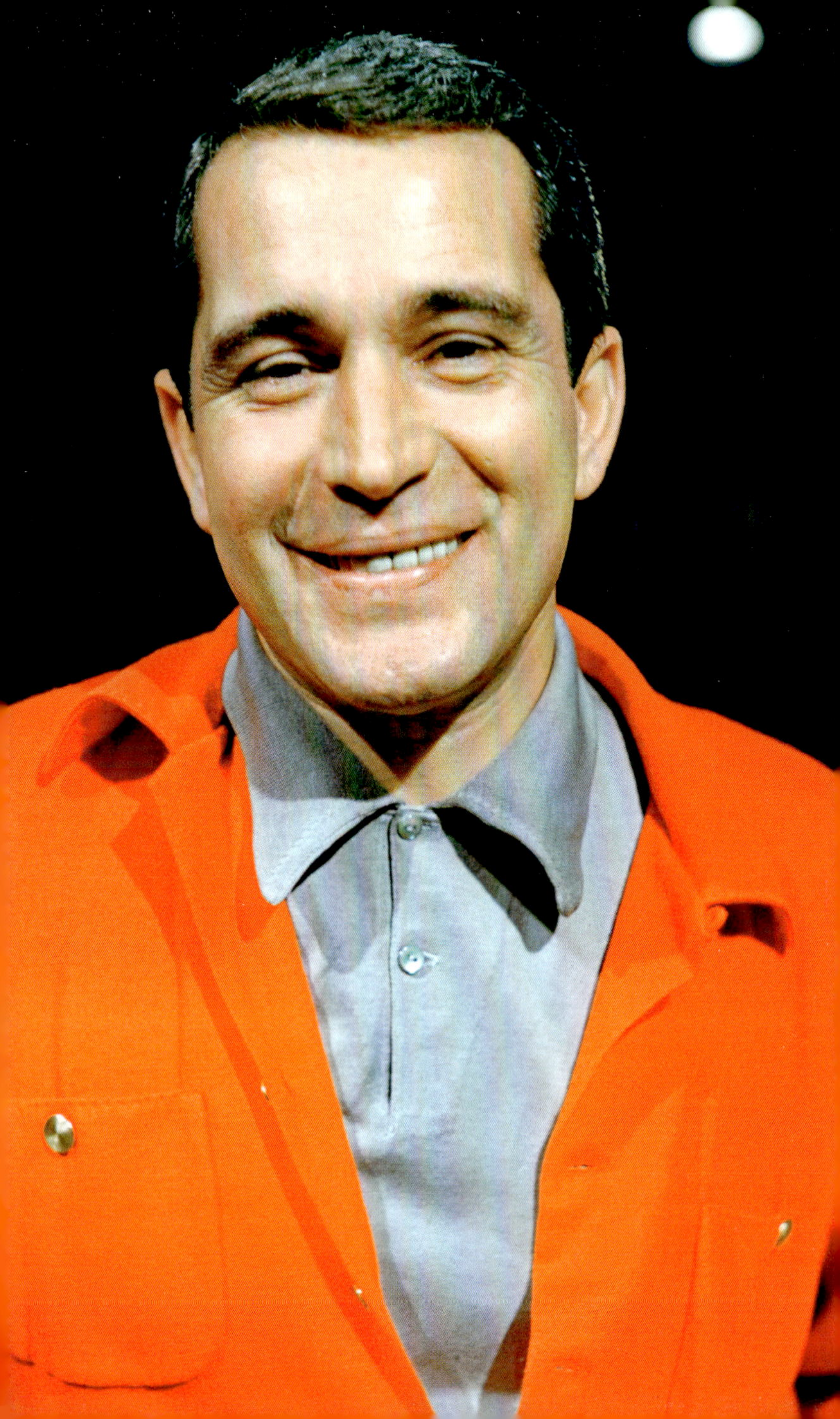

# Hair

From day one, hair has always been of huge importance to the Mod. The first style the Mods latched onto was called the Perry Como. Como was an Italian-American singer who had left school to work in a barbershop. He later turned to singing, and his easygoing vocal style and character brought him a huge middle-aged audience. (Later on in life Como often wore cardigans on his hugely popular TV show. These became known as Perry Como sweaters and account for the derision Mods received when they wore cardigans.) Como's haircut was Italian. The hair was cut short all round with a parting on either side, a style which required no grease or oil. Mods liked this style but then some moved onto the college boy look. The college boy cut (styled famously by American president John F. Kennedy) was shorter than Como's but with the same parting. The French crop also proved successful: it was basically the crew cut of the

*Opposite:* The haircut that inspired a movement, sported by the man himself: singer Perry Como, seen here *circa* 1955

If you can't beat them, join them: a young Mod girl gets a 'boy's' haircut in a barbers on London's Walworth Road

American Marines but was worn a little bit longer. As Mods grew in number, the bouffant style, a French creation, also found a lot of takers. This saw Mods grow their hair longer and thicker and then create a bouffant at the back of the head, with a small parting placed in front of it. In 1966 a new generation of Mods emerged who wore very severe crew cuts. They were called Hard Mods and it was this style that would later be picked up by the Mod's second cousin, the Skinhead.

H

The head college boy: the 35th President of the United States, John F. Kennedy, in 1963

# Irish Jack

Irish Jack on a Lambretta Special X 200

Jack Lyons was born in Cork, Ireland, in 1943, and grew up in the Shepherd's Bush area of London. In 1962, at the local Goldhawk Social Club, he witnessed a live set from a band called The Detours. Jack loved them and quickly befriended the band, in particular their guitarist, Pete Townshend. The Detours went on to become The Who and Jack Lyons became 'Irish Jack', a name given to him by the band's co-manager Kit Lambert. Jack would later be considered the unofficial fifth member of the group. As The Who went on to achieve superstardom, Jack returned to Cork, where he has remained to this day, first working as a bus conductor and then as a postman. In 1973 The Who released the album *Quadrophenia*, the name derived from the term schizophrenia, reflecting the four personalities of Jimmy, the main character on the record (see *Quadrophenia* – The Film). Townshend quickly acknowledged Irish Jack as the main inspiration for the work, which immediately elevated Lyons to cult status. Since then he has given talks and interviews on the subject all over the world and has featured in books. He still keeps in regular contact with Townshend and Roger Daltrey and he was guest of honour at the band's gig in Cork in 2007 where, at the end of the performance, Daltrey shouted from the stage: 'Look after yer postman!'

*Top:* Close up of Jack Lyons

*Bottom left:* Jack in The Marquee Club, 1966

*Bottom right:* Jack on the Vespa GS ridden by Sting in the film *Quadrophenia*

# The Isle of Wight Scooter Rally

Each year, over the August bank holiday weekend, thousands of Mods and scooterists gather at the Isle of Wight for one of the country's biggest rallies. This annual pilgrimage attracts over 6,000 bikes from all over the world. Others arrive by car or on foot, attracted by club nights, well-known DJs, live concerts and numerous record stalls, plus the special scooter events that are held in and around the area of Ryde.

Scooter rallies have been popular in the UK since the 1950s, when both Lambretta and Vespa machines proved highly desirable. In the early 1960s Mods chose the scooter as their transport of choice and these vehicles became an integral part of their lifestyle. With the Mod revival of the late 1970s, the scooterist culture became massive, with hundreds of clubs springing up, a trend that continues to this day. Due to the numbers that attend the Isle of Wight, accommodation is at a premium. Over 2,000 people camp at the Smallbrook Stadium, with B&Bs and hotels often fully booked. The main ride-out, in which the majority of the bikes take part, takes place on Sunday, the scooters all leaving around 1 p.m.

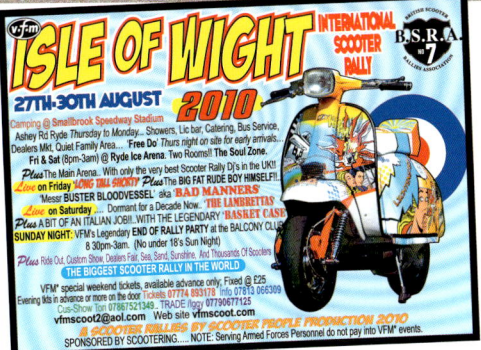

*Top:* A trio of highly accessorised scooters stand to be admired at the Isle of Wight gathering of 2011

*Bottom:* Flyer for the 2010 Isle of Wight rally

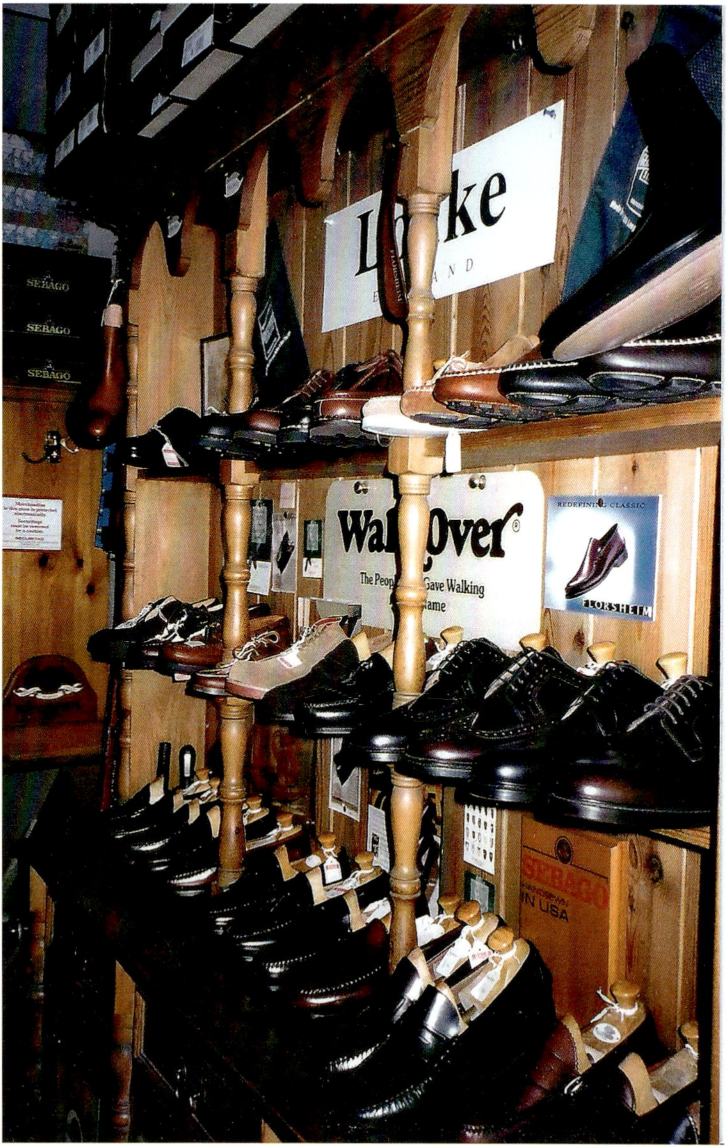

# The Ivy Shop

Opened in the summer of 1965 by John Simons and his then business partner Jeff Kwintner, The Ivy Shop at 10 Hill Rise, Richmond, specialised in the American Ivy League style and so became the holy grail for many stylists.

The Ivy League in the USA comprises eight private 'schools': Yale, Harvard, Brown, Columbia, Cornell, Dartmouth, Princeton and the University of Pennsylvania. The students on campus of the late 1950s and early 1960s developed a very distinctive, conservative form of dress which crossed over to the general public and made its way to the UK in the early 1960s.

Simons's idea was to sell this clothing to British executives, thus giving them the chance to dress like their American contemporaries. Simons had long been a Modernist. As a kid he had seen an American soldier dressed in gabardine trousers with shiny brogues and had been transfixed by American clothing ever since. Early photos

*Opposite:* These shoes were made for walking: a fine selection of brogues and loafers for sale in the original Ivy Shop

*Top:* John Simons, co-founder and owner of the The Ivy Shop, in the early 1960s

Richmond, England. The front of The Ivy Shop in the 1980s

of Simons reveal a young man dressing well ahead of his time in his sheepskin coats and two-button jackets. He attended concerts at the Lyceum in the early 1950s and saw the Modernist movement turn into Mod. The Ivy League look became a real passion for him and so on opening day he was shocked and then pleasantly surprised to find his shop overrun by Mods. They were there to explore the treasure trove of American clothing, with Simons and Kwintner selling shirts by the likes of Lion of Troy and Albany and jackets by Baracuta. There were chino trousers and Levi's' Sta-Prest. There were American wing-tip brogues and later the Bass Weejun loafer in all its glorious forms, including the Beef Roll, the Tassel and the Penny (see Bass Weejuns). The arrival of Madras cotton shirts also made a huge impact.

After nearly 30 years of service, the shop closed on 21 January 1995. It was the end of an era – but not of the man. Simons opened up J. Simons in Covent Garden, where he successfully operated for many years before switching to his current location at 46 Chiltern Street, London W1.

John Simon and friends in 1950s London

# ronnie scott's

**J**

It's 1963 and Ronnie Scott and saxophonist Roland Kirk relax outside the original Ronnie Scott's, situated at 39 Gerard Street in London's Chinatown. The club opened in 1959 with the great Tubby Hayes as the opening act

# Jazz Style

In 1948 the young jazz musician Ronnie Scott and ten of his friends opened Club Eleven on Soho's Great Windmill Street. The setting was very basic – a basement with a small makeshift stage – but the music was fervently Modernist, with Scott and his boys playing bebop to a hip clientele until the morning light. Jazz was London's major music and it was split into two camps: the Modernists and the trad jazzers, who listened to 1920s New Orleans music. Trad jazz's cheerful disposition and undemanding structures were anathema to the likes of Scott, who much preferred the challenging sounds of Charlie Parker, Dizzy Gillespie, Chet Baker, Miles Davis *et al*. In honour of these transatlantic heroes, Ronnie and his boys sought to dress like them.

Of all the American jazzers, Miles Davis was the coolest, the leader of the pack. Davis did not just wear clothes but used them, just as he used

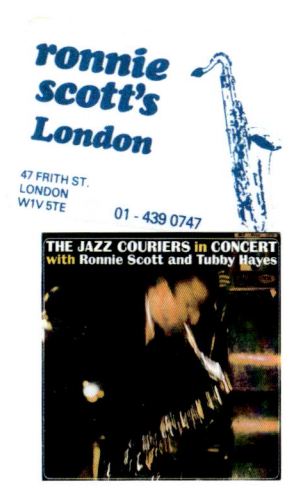

*Top:* Membership card for Ronnie Scott's club, 1985

*Bottom:* Album cover of *The Jazz Couriers in Concert*, featuring Ronnie Scott and Tubby Hayes, 1958

*Main:* Tubby Hayes performing at the BBC TV Centre, 1965

*Inset:* Miles Davis in 'that green shirt' on the cover of his album *Milestones*, 1958

his trumpet. For Davis, clothes provided disguise, perfect to infiltrate the mainstream with. He loved the idea that people passing him on the street, taking in his immaculate suit, pressed white shirt, beautifully knotted tie and shiny brogue shoes, would think him an office clerk. They would not have an inkling that he was on the way to the studio to create revolutionary and radical music that would help liberate people's minds. In the 1950s Davis loved the Brooks Brothers look but his travels to Europe also brought a Continental element to his style, and he added cravats and handkerchiefs, to great effect. His influence on the London jazz scene, which had much to do with kickstarting the initial Mod movement, was massive.

In the 1950s the likes of Tubby Hayes, Stan Tracey and Phil Seamen dominated the British jazz scene and did so in stylish suits and sunglasses. These guys were the template for the North London youth who in 1958 adopted the Modernist tag and ran with it so successfully.

*Top:* Stan Tracey and Lucky Thompson performing with the band, 1962

*Bottom:* Miles in a lovely double-breasted suit, showing his undoubted style nous

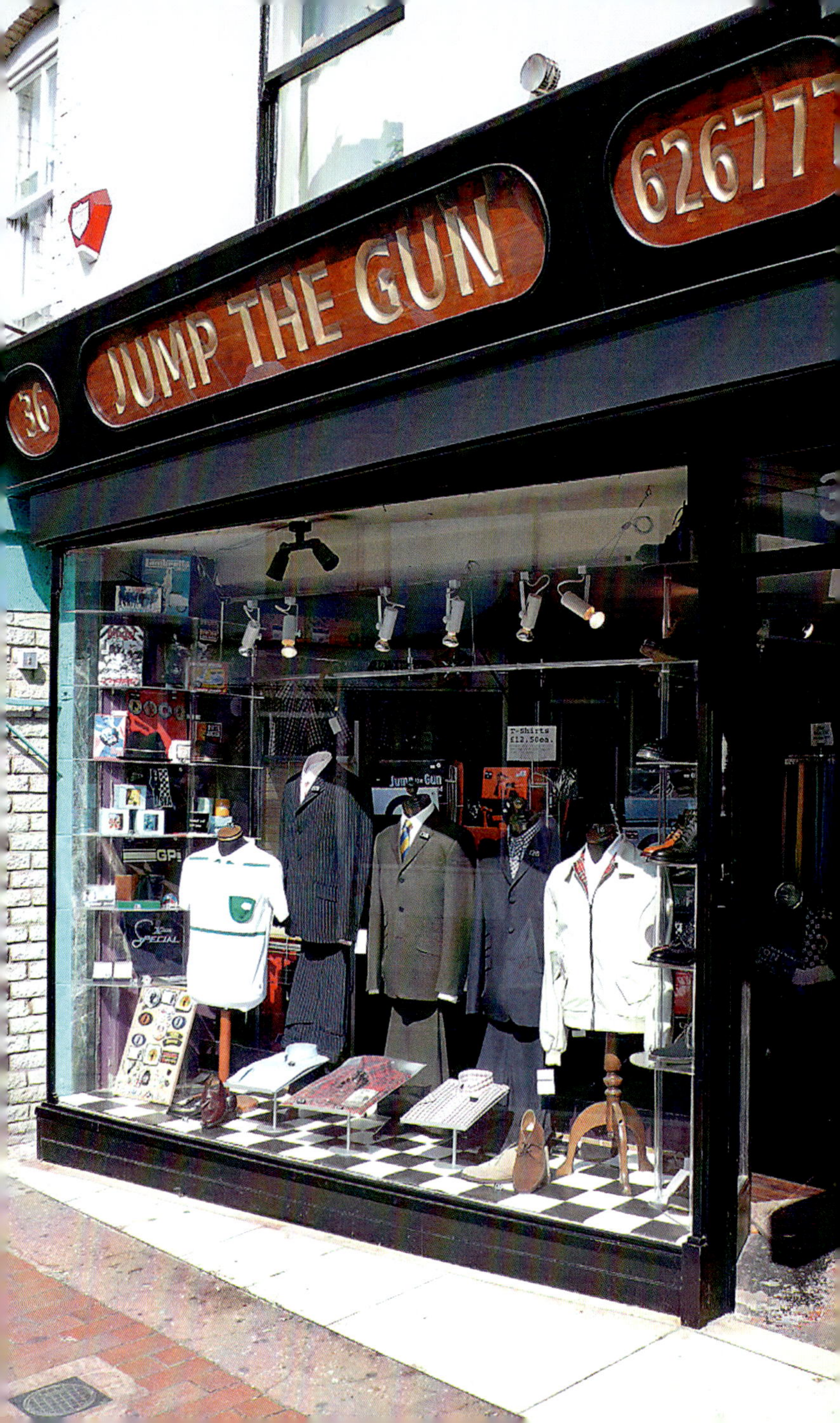
36
JUMP THE GUN
62677

# Jump the Gun

The two Le Roy brothers, Adam and his elder brother Jonathan, grew up in and around the Hampstead area of London. In 1982 they got into the Mod/scooter scene and started printing and selling tee-shirts at various street markets. In the early 1990s they decided to try their luck in Brighton. They found empty premises on Gardner Street and opened a shop in 1992, naming it in honour of an old ska track called 'Jumping the Gun', which was a particular favourite of theirs at that time. As confirmed Mods, it made sense for them to stock clothing which reflected their lifestyle. Before long, rails of Lonsdale and Ben Sherman clothing lined the shop. At first the shop struggled to compete against the US street labels that dominated retail at the time, but with the advent of Britpop, the boys found themselves in

*Opposite:* Jump the Gun shopfront and window display, Brighton, summer 2011

*Top:* Jump the Gun logo

*Bottom:* Adam and Jonathan Le Roy, owners and co-founders

*Top:* Interior of the shop

*Opposite:* Promotional advertising for Jump the Gun's own clothing brand

the right place, at the right time, with the right stock. Business boomed and they have never looked back. Twenty years on, they design and manufacture the vast majority of their clothing, with suits, shirts and knitwear all made to very high standards, their designs a nod to the years between 1959 and 1962. Their garments are sold in the UK and all over the world. Jump the Gun have succeeded because they instinctively believe what all Mods do: that 1960s cool will forever endure.

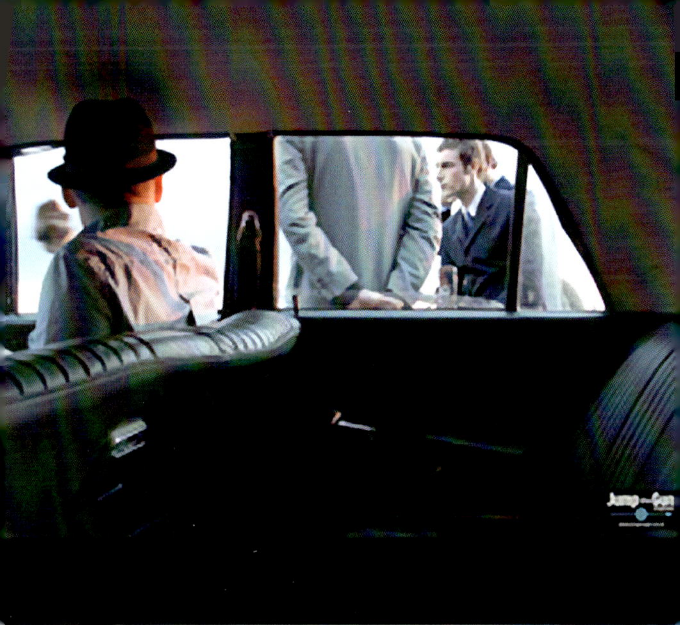

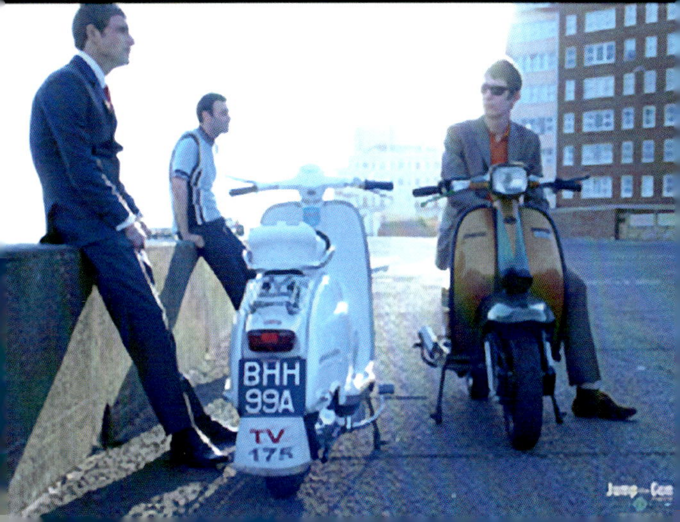
BHH
99A
TV
175

*Top:* Album cover of *Smart! – 16 Immaculate Cuts Tailored for Style* on the Kent label

*Bottom left:* The label for 'Hey Stoney Face' by Mary Love, issued for the 5th anniversary of The 6Ts' all-nighters, run by Kent Records head honcho Ady Croasdell

*Bottom right:* Flyer promoting the 1997 Cleethorpes Weekender

152

# Kent Records

Started in 1982 by Ady Croasdell, Kent Records has proved to be one of Britain's most enduring record labels, a highly important label for turning on budding Modernists to the glories of black American music. It has also acted as a godsend for those seeking rare tunes with only coins in their pockets. Seen primarily as a Northern Soul label, Kent's remit is actually much wider. Many of their compilations contain not just soul stompers but all kinds of different music, from harmony to tough r'n'b, pop soul and deep ballads. It has also issued fine compilations of Mod-based acts such as The Impressions, Mary Love and the titanic soul duo Eddie and Ernie, as well as giving the world Dave Godin's wonderful *Deep Soul* series. Despite the excellence of their back catalogue, the Kent team remain adamant that there is still much more wonderful soul music to uncover and unleash.

Album cover of *Think Smart*

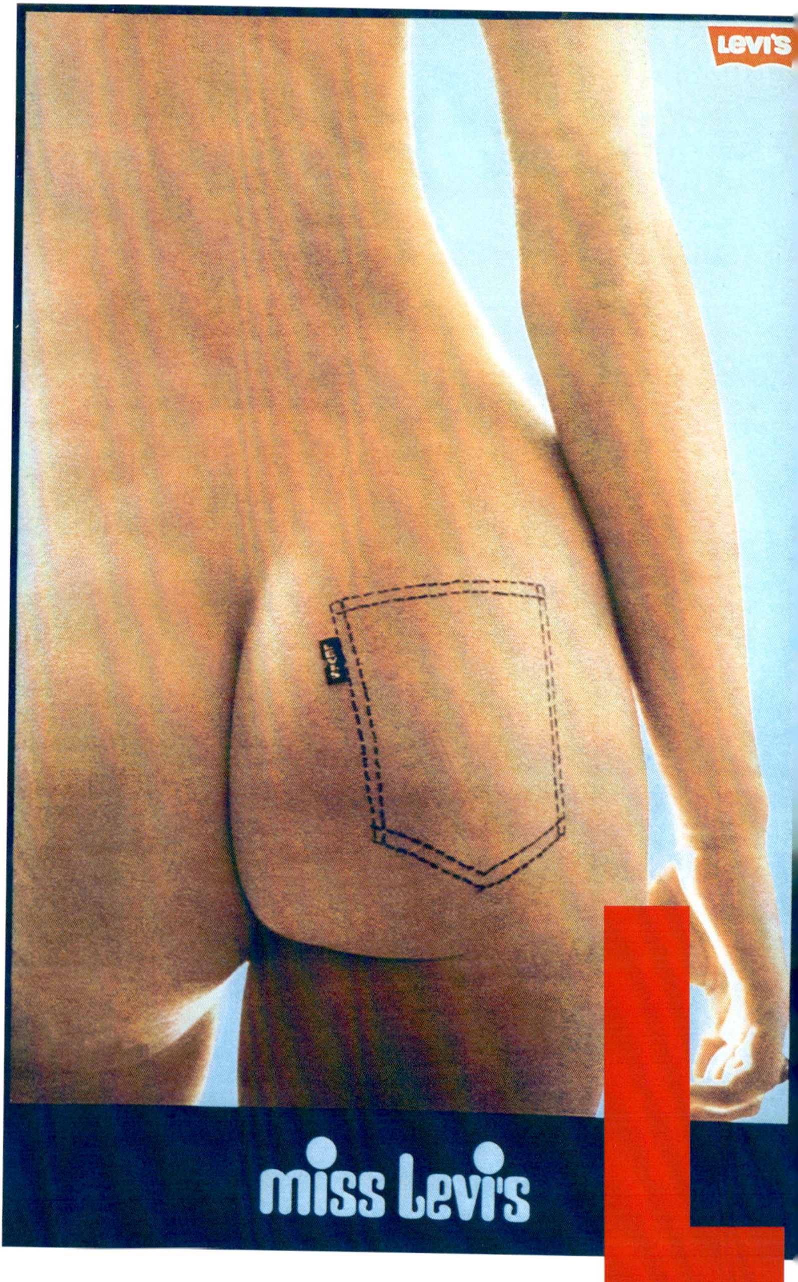
Levi's
miss Levi's

# Levi's Jeans

The original, strict Mod look was diluted in the early 1960s and was replaced by a casual style. One of the leading components of this look was a pair of Levi's 501 shrink-to-fit denim jeans. Getting hold of a pair was the first trick since, from the 1950s onwards, they were notoriously hard to track down on the streets of the UK. Rumours would spread of one or two shops that stocked them (indeed, Marc Bolan once boasted that he and his friends robbed 40 pairs in an East End warehouse one night), but once word went around they were soon sold out. However, there was always a plentiful supply at the PX stores on the US military bases in the UK. PX stood for Post Exchange, a retail store within the base where servicemen could buy civilian clothing. Local musicians entertaining the troops would always stock up on jeans, and some of the black GIs who frequented the Soho clubs of the time began a roaring trade in selling Levi's to Mods desperate

*Opposite:* Magazine advert for Miss Levi's

*Top:* A stack of Levi's jeans

Breast pocket of a suede Levi's 'Vintage' jacket

to get their hands on the real deal. The image of a Mod sitting in the bath attempting the 'shrink-to-fit' technique was memorably captured in the 1979 film *Quadrophenia*, featuring Phil Daniels as Jimmy. Paul Weller of The Jam often wore his with an inch-high turn-up and in the 1980s only those Levi's with red stitching could be worn by discerning Mods.

The actual story of the Levi Strauss company begins in old Bavaria, which Strauss left in 1853 to set up business in San Francisco. He was approached by local tailor Jacob Davis to go into business together in 1873, with Davis making work clothes and dungarees from the bolts of cloth that Strauss sold from his wholesale dry goods store. Davis had the idea of adding rivets to areas of the clothes that were continually being torn, such as the corners of pockets. Sales of denim trousers began in the 1920s, but purely to the working man: railway workers, cowboys and so on. Jeans as we know them today became a fashion item in the 1950s, crossing over worldwide through various youth cults from the 1960s onwards. Levi Strauss & Co. is still privately owned by the descendants of the Strauss family and 501s remain one of its most popular brands.

An advertisement for Levi Strauss & Co.'s copper-riveted overalls, *circa* 1875. The hard-wearing garments were very popular with miners in the American West

French pop singer Sylvie Vartan visits Cathy on the set of *Ready, Steady, Go!*, November 1965

# Cathy McGowan

The 19-year-old Cathy McGowan was working in the fashion department of the magazine *Woman's Own* when in 1963 she answered an advert for a presenter on a new TV pop show called *Ready, Steady, Go!* Her natural style and good looks saw her beat 600 other applicants to land the job. *Ready, Steady, Go!* became an overnight sensation, presenting music in a fresh and innovative way. The calibre of the acts that appeared on the show – The Small Faces, The Who, James Brown and Otis Redding, to name but a few – and the fact that many of its audience and dancers were selected from Mod clubs ensured that the show picked up a healthy Mod following. One side effect of its success was that the fashions displayed on the show spread nationally, thus creating a nationwide Mod movement. McGowan's catchphrases 'Smashing' and 'Fab', coupled with her natural fashion sense, meant she was soon christened

Cathy McGowan, *circa* 1966

*Top:* McGowan modelling clothes at the Royal College of Art, June 1966

*Opposite:* 'The Queen of the Mods' looking fab!

the 'Queen of the Mods' by the media. Hyperbole perhaps, but with so few women in the Mod movement, McGowan was an important figure for the girl followers of the scene. Within a few months, she was presenting her own show for Radio Luxembourg, writing newspaper and magazine columns and launching her own fashion range at British Home Stores. She married actor Hywel Bennett (*The Family Way*) in 1970. However, once *Ready, Steady, Go!* had finished her career took a dip. Over the next few years she worked on the board of Capital Radio and did stints on other TV shows, and also concentrated on charity work.

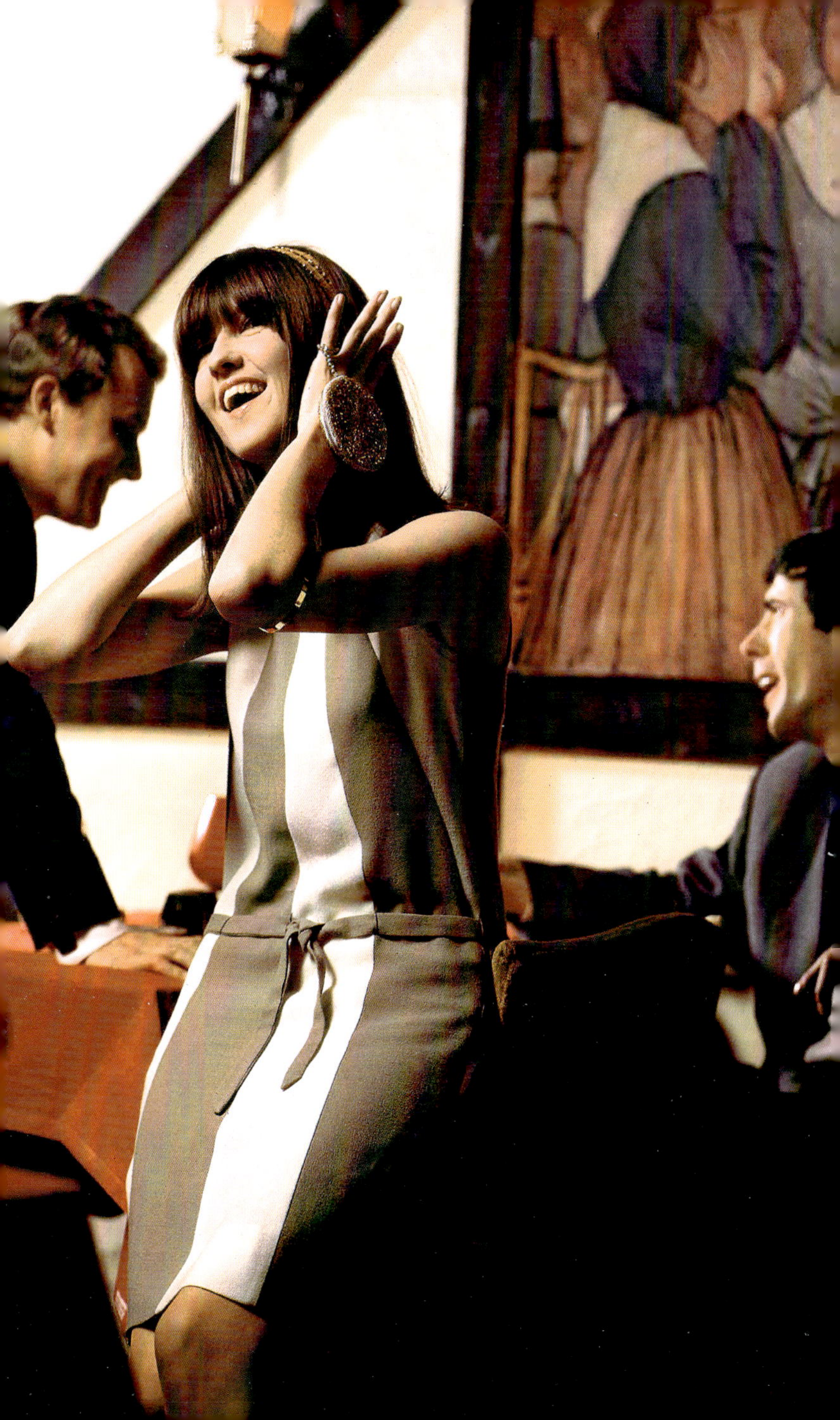

Clean Living under difficult circumstances.

# Pete Meaden

Many can still picture him buzzing around the West End of London, stomach full of pills, head full of plans, looking for that one idea that will spark up and set his world ablaze. He was one of Mod's greatest ambassadors. Peter – forever known as Pete – Meaden was born in 1941. It was perfect timing. When the first wave of Mods hit London in the late 1950s, Meaden was in pole position. He had left school and found work as a freelance publicist for visiting American musicians such as Chuck Berry and homegrown talent like The Rolling Stones. By night he could be found at The Scene Club in Ham Yard, soaking up the sights and sounds. He lived in a room on Monmouth Street, bang in the centre of town. It is said that his possessions consisted of a collection of vinyl on the Sue label, a Dansette to play them on and an ironing board; a proper Mod, then. He also began a short-lived Mod fanzine with Andrew Loog Oldham.

*Opposite:* The wise words of Mr Meaden

One day his barber, Jack, mentioned to him a band called The Who. When Meaden checked them out, he instantly saw the perfect opportunity to create a proper London Mod band. He befriended the group, became their manager and changed everything about them – their hair, their clothes, their attitude. He changed their name to The High Numbers and got them gigs. He also wrote them two songs which he ripped off from black American rhythm and blues records, 'I'm the Face' with 'Zoot Suit'; the B-side was the band's first single. Unfortunately for Meaden, Kit Lambert and his partner Chris Stamp came looking for a band to film. They saw The Who, fell in love with them and ended up buying them from Meaden for £500. He later found out they had been prepared to give him £5,000.

*Opposite:* An early PR client of Pete Meaden, rock'n'roller Chuck Berry, seen here in 1958

Meaden managed Mod fave band Jimmy James and the Vagabonds, with limited success.

M

He had been given Drynamil by his GP back in 1962 to counter anxiety attacks and the years of popping pills and life on the road started to take a toll on his already fragile mind. He was later to spend time in and out of mental institutions. He believed that the character of Jimmy from *Quadrophenia* was based on him. He also worked with the Steve Gibbons Band.

Pete Meaden died aged 36 in July 1978 in a bedroom in his parents' house in Edmonton, North London, where he had dreamt up the name The High Numbers and written the lyrics to 'I'm the Face'. In a memorable interview from the mid-1970s with journalist Steve Turner of the *NME* he coined the phrase that will forever be his epitaph. When asked to define Mod he simply replied, 'Clean living under difficult circumstances.'

*Opposite:* An article on Meaden from the magazine *Boyfriend*

IF you haunt the London clubs like the 'Scene' and the 'Flamingo', then don't be surprised if this week's Undiscovered British Boyfriend looks vaguely familiar to you. For 21-year-old Peter Meaden admits he's more often out enjoying the London night life than at home! And this isn't only because he likes the clubs—although that's true, too—but because Peter is one of the behind-the-scene boys in the pop world, and he thinks it's disastrous for anyone in the pop world to get out of touch with the trends. Actually, Peter is one of the people who set them. You've probably heard a lot about tickets and faces lately, well, Peter's a face!

Auburn-haired and blue-eyed, Peter's just a fraction under 6 ft. He was at grammar school and then he left for art school with five 'O' levels and two 'A's to his credit. Art school lasted about one year! Later, Peter had left both school and home for a flat in Hampstead and a job in an advertising agency.

After that—another agency. Then he joined up with Andrew Oldham (the Stones' manager) to form an advertising agency, until last year when he left the country for seven months. After making some money in Spain and North Africa—'something to do with cars'—Peter arrived back in England and almost immediately flew off for a vacation in America for three weeks. He gets around, this boy!

Back from the States, Peter tried his hand as a free-lance photographer and journalist for a while, then finally joined up again with his old partner Andrew Oldham, handling publicity for the Crystals, Gene Pitney and the Stones.

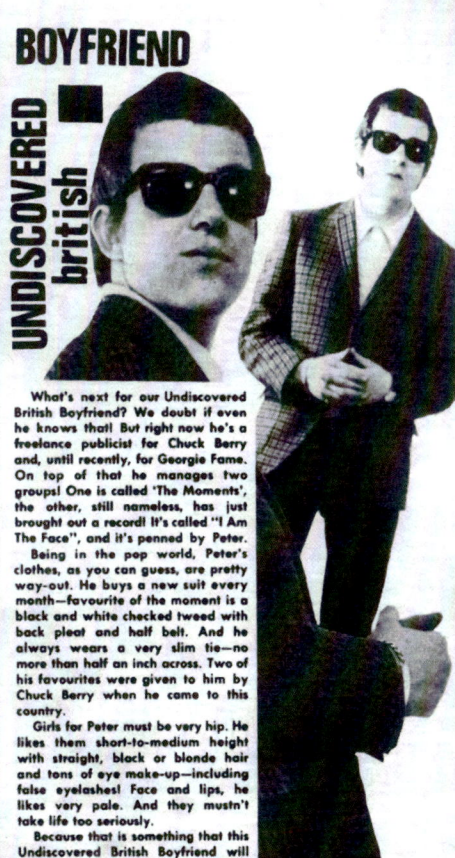

# BOYFRIEND

## UNDISCOVERED british

What's next for our Undiscovered British Boyfriend? We doubt if even he knows that! But right now he's a freelance publicist for Chuck Berry and, until recently, for Georgie Fame. On top of that he manages two groups! One is called 'The Moments', the other, still nameless, has just brought out a record! It's called "I Am The Face", and it's penned by Peter.

Being in the pop world, Peter's clothes, as you can guess, are pretty way-out. He buys a new suit every month—favourite of the moment is a black and white checked tweed with back pleat and half belt. And he always wears a very slim tie—no more than half an inch across. Two of his favourites were given to him by Chuck Berry when he came to this country.

Girls for Peter must be very hip. He likes them short-to-medium height with straight, black or blonde hair and tons of eye make-up—including false eyelashes! Face and lips, he likes very pale. And they mustn't take life too seriously.

Because that is something that this Undiscovered British Boyfriend will never do!

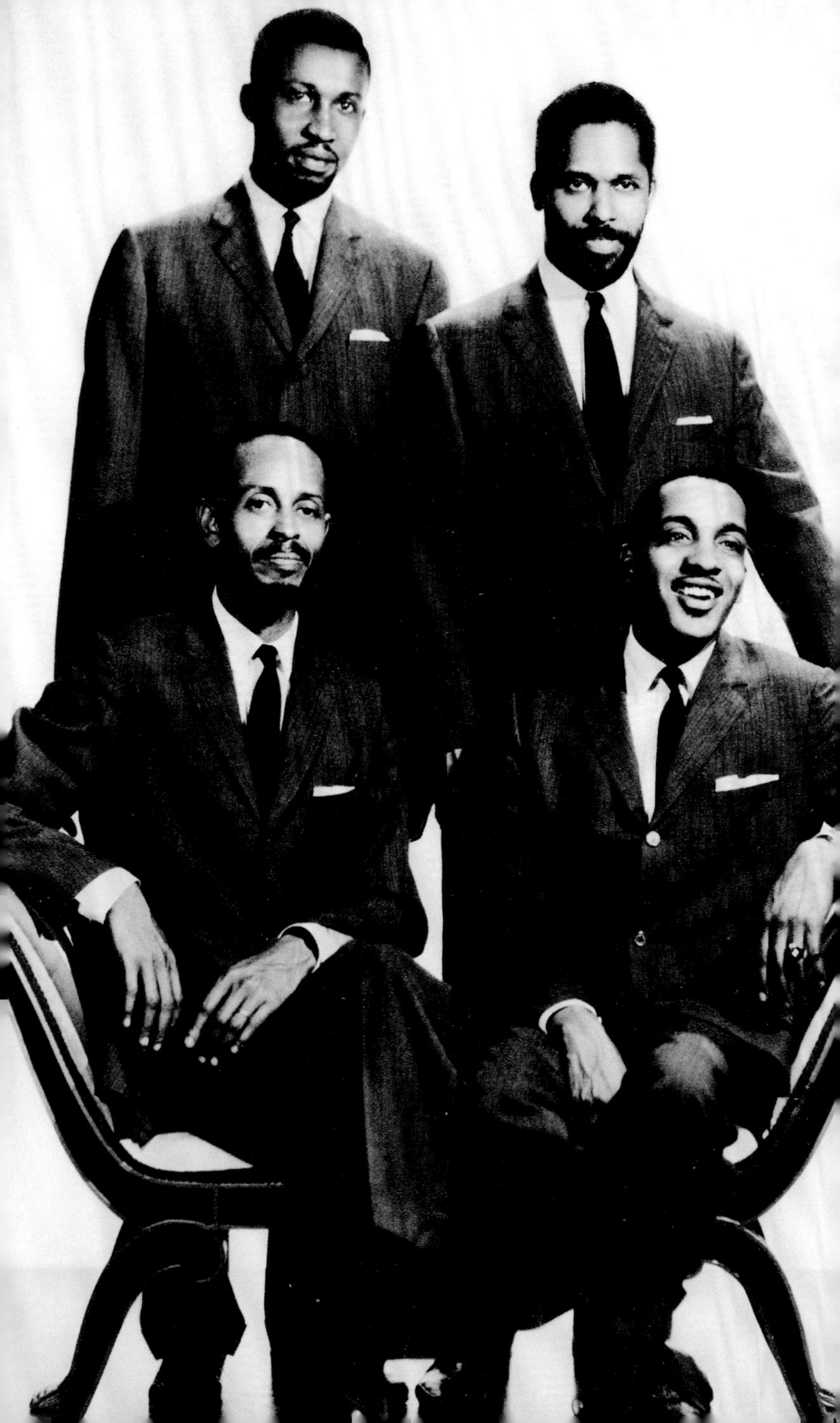

# Modern Jazz Quartet

Cool and sharp – if any musical group sum up these two words, then it is the Modern Jazz Quartet. Formed in 1952 and comprising John Lewis on piano, Milt Jackson on vibes, Kenny Clarke on drums (replaced by Connie Kay in 1955) and Percy Heath on bass, MJQ were the epitome of understated, delicate jazz. Their unique sound was said to 'combine Bach with Charlie Parker' and proved highly successful. Their debut album, *MJQ*, released by Prestige in the year of their formation, was a huge success for the label, and the group's popularity never waned throughout the next 15 years or so. Their style caught the eyes and ears of British jazz players such as Tubby Hayes, who cited Milt Jackson as a major influence upon his work. MJQ albums such as *Place Vendôme*, recorded in Paris in 1966 with The Swingle Singers, showed the dexterity of their collective techniques. Signed to Atlantic Records for most of their

*Opposite:* MJQ – nice! From top left clockwise: John Lewis, Connie Kay, Milt Jackson and Percy Heath pose in 1960

*Top:* Album cover of *Place Vendôme* by MJQ and The Swingle Singers

MJQ, 1970

career, the band enjoyed a brief spell with The Beatles' label, Apple. After several well-received albums, Jackson left the band in 1974, and rather than replace the irreplaceable, the group simply disbanded. They later re-formed in 1981 and toured extensively. Around this time they were cited as a musical and fashion influence by Paul Weller. The band's penchant for wearing MJQ patches on the top pockets of their smart blazers was copied by The Style Council in their early years. The band's last recording was in 1993 and Percy Heath, the last surviving member, died in 2005. In over 40 years MJQ never missed a gig or disappointed an audience. Moreover, they remained highly stylish to the end.

The Modern Jazz Quartet perform at the Birdland Jazz Club in New York, 1954. L to R: Jackson on vibes, Lewis at the piano, Heath on bass and Kay on drums

MADE IN ENGL...

BILGORRI
THE SPORTSMAN'S TAILO...
189/191, BISHOPSGATE, E.C...
PHONE BIS 7702

ACE FACE
CLOTHING CO.

The Original Two-Tone Iridescent To...
www.acefaceclothingcompany.com
Telephone : 01342 835447

KID MOHAIR AN...

KID MOHAIR MADE

ACE FAC...

# Mohair

Mohair is the material of Mods. It is perfect for both dancing and posing in – two activities in which Mods specialise. Mohair is made from the hair of the Angora goat and since the Second World War has been the first choice of cool jazzers and hot soul singers. Musicians such as Miles Davis, Chet Baker, Wilson Pickett and vocal bands like The Drifters and The Impressions have all appeared on album sleeves dressed in sharp mohair suits. These suits were intensely studied by London Mods and then copied.

The most popular styles of mohair are two-ply, three-ply and Tonik, the last produced by the French firm Dormeuil. This fabric became especially popular in the early 1970s among the Suedehead movement. Today Tonik is best sourced from The Ace Face Clothing Company, which tracked down the original material and are able to create bespoke suits from it.

*Opposite (L to R clockwise):* Blue mohair; a wooden clothes hanger from legendary tailor Bilgorri, who was based in Bishopgate in the East End of London; purple kid mohair; bronze 3-ply mohair; brown mohair; the Ace Face Clothing label

*Bottom:* A mohair swatch book for the company Bateman Ogden

# Motown

Such is its power that Motown Records has become embedded in the fabric of all our lives, not just the Mod brotherhood. Yet it was the Mods who first latched onto Motown music and paved the way for its acceptance in the UK. Motown was started in Detroit in 1959 by a 23-year-old ex-boxer named Berry Gordy Junior. Gordy had already had a taste of musical success. He had co-written the hits 'Reet Petite' and 'Lonely Teardrops' for singer Jackie Wilson. In 1957 he began Tamla Records, releasing records by artists such as Marv Johnson and a young vocal group called The Miracles, whose leader was the highly talented singer-songwriter Smokey Robinson. In 1959 Gordy launched Motown Records, taking the name from Detroit's nickname, 'Motor Town', which it had garnered due to its huge car industry. The label operated out of 2648 West Grand Boulevard, later dubbed Hitsville, USA.

*Top:* The single 'Wherever I Lay My Hat' by Marvin Gaye, 1962

*Bottom:* Smokey Robinson and the Miracles, *circa* 1965

The founder of Motown,
Mr Berry Gordy, 1965

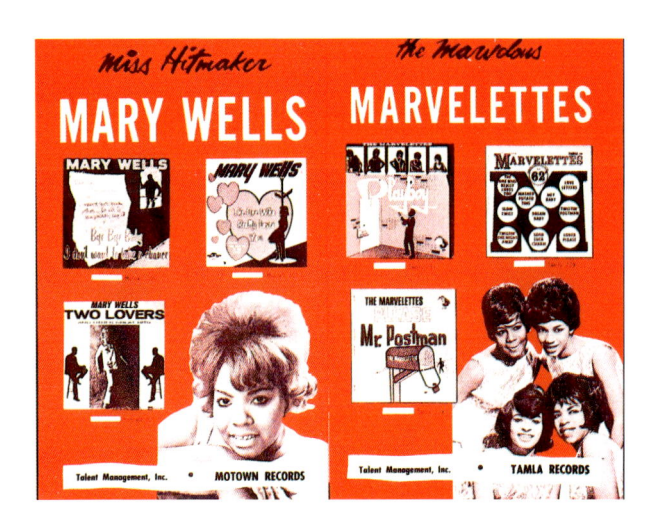

Gordy, who had worked on car lines, set his label up on a similar pattern. He brought in songwriters who would have to compete with each other to have their songs placed with acts. Otherwise they went unpaid. Eventually, Holland, Dozier and Holland became Motown's most prolific songwriting team, with talents such as Smokey Robinson not far behind.

The acts themselves were carefully controlled in what they wore and how they carried themselves in public. Gordy was determined to cross over to a white audience and much of the music he released was radio-friendly, with high commercial and artistic values. Motown records were perfect for dancing to, relying on an infectious drum beat and driving instrumentation. In the UK imports of these records were eagerly tracked down and many Tamla-Motown records became dance-floor favourites in the Mod clubs of the day.

*Top:* Motown adverts for 'Miss Hitmaker Mary Wells' and 'The Marvelous Marvelettes'

*Opposite:* The genius born Stevland Hardaway Judkins/Morris but better known to the world as Stevie Wonder, 1965

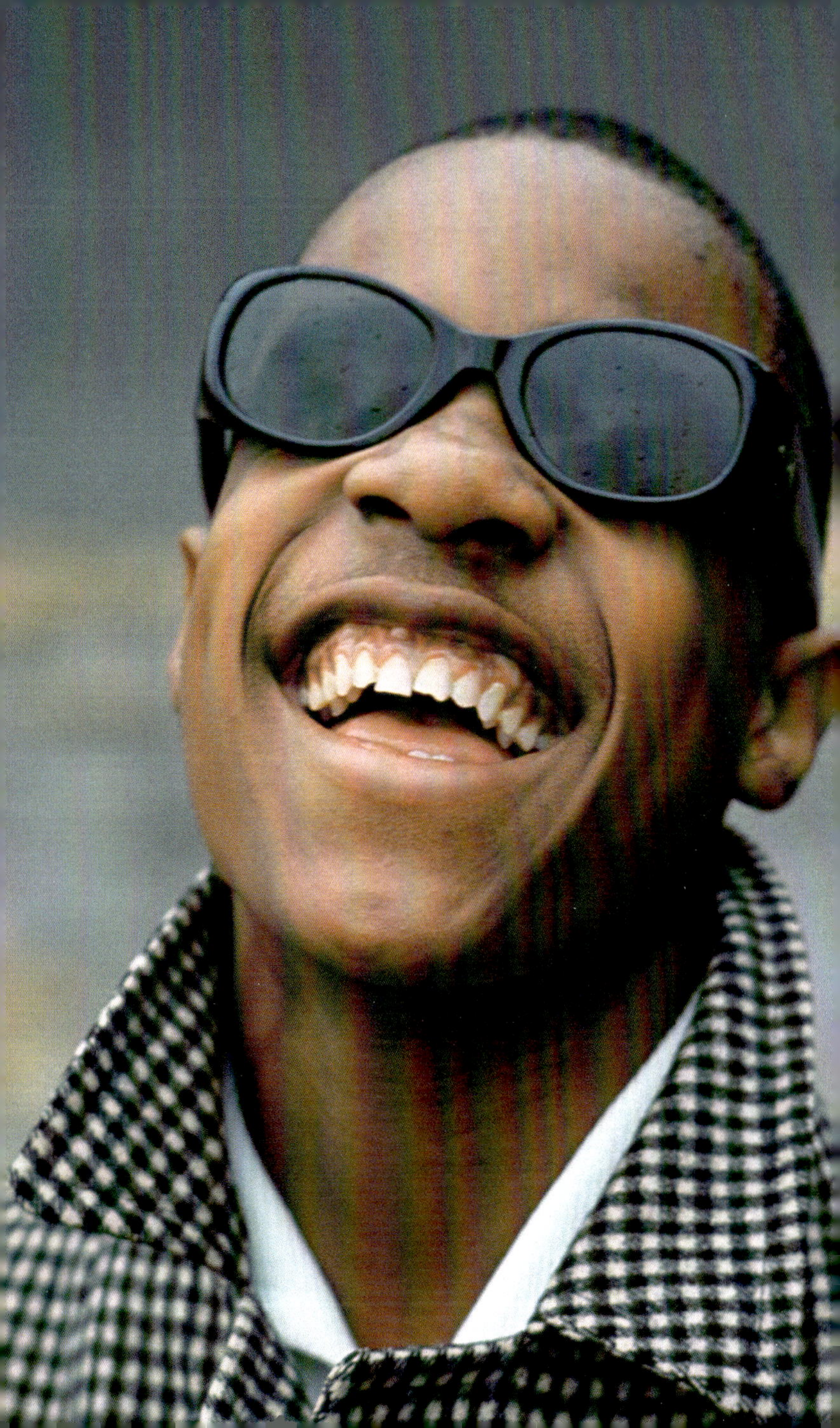

The mighty Supremes in 1964. L to R: Diana Ross, Mary Wilson and group founder Florence Ballard

(When asked, leading 1960s Mod Richard Barnes often nominates Martha and the Vandellas' 'Dancing In the Street' as the ultimate Mod record.) There are simply too many Motown Mod tunes to list here but any top 100 Mod chart will always contain a healthy sprinkling of them. In 1965 the television show *Ready, Steady, Go!* devoted a whole show to Motown music, with singer Dusty Springfield (herself a keen enthusiast) hosting the event. Motown's ability to unearth talent was unsupassed. The list includes legendary names such as Martha and the Vandellas, Stevie Wonder, Marvin Gaye, The Supremes, The Four Tops, Junior Walker and the All-Stars, The Temptations, Gladys Knight and the Pips and The Jackson Five. From 1961 to 1971 Motown scored over 110 top ten hits.

In 1972 Gordy relocated the company to Los Angeles and diversified into areas such as film. The company, while never matching its incredible early output, still score many chart hits. But in 1988 Gordy retired and sold the company to MCA Records. His Jobette publishing company went to EMI. The Universal Music Group now owns the back catalogue. Asked if he felt as if he had failed by selling the company. Gordy replied: 'I have just made over $300 million today. What do you think?'

Lost in the moment: A Northern Soul dancer, 1975

**6 T's RHYTHM N' SOUL CLU**
are WILDLY HAPPY TO ANNOUNCE
we are RE-OPENIN
MEMBERSHIP TO
OUR FORTNIGHTLY PURE SOUL
DANCES
at STARLIGHT ROOM
THE RAILWAY HOTEL, 100 WES
END LANE
WEST HAMPSTEAD (by tube) NW

Next Date is SATURDAY, AUGUST 23. 7.45-12.15
then SATURDAY, SEPTEMBER 6
(and every 2 weeks thereafter)
Admittance is to MEMBERS ONLY
Membership is £1.00 with an SAE to ADRIAN CROASDE
FLAT 5, 52 LANGHAM STREET, LONDON W1
(That also includes the monthly newsletter)
Sounds by Maxine Brown, Spooner's Crowd, Impressio
Chuck Jackson, Solomon Burke, Jewels (Dimensions), N
Simone and their chums
DJ's are: TONY ROUNCE * TONY ELLIS * IAN CLA
RANDY COZENS * MICK SMITH and PETE WIDDIS
The Crowd is Knowledgeable and Friendly

# Northern Soul

The best youth trends exist for years before the media discover them and in doing so ring their death knell. So it was with Mod, and so it was with Northern Soul. Northern Soul grew out of the dying embers of the Mod world when in 1967 soul music headed north, and located itself at Manchester's Twisted Wheel club. Here DJ Roger Eagle played a mouthwatering set of American rhythm and blues while presenting a number of live acts, including Junior Walker and the All-Stars. The style of dancing that originated here led to the unique moves that would characterise Northern Soul clubs in the 1970s.

Blighted by non-stop drug raids, The Twisted Wheel was finally forced to close in 1971. In its place came a host of clubs dotted around the North, including The Golden Torch in Stoke, The Mecca in Blackpool and, later, the scene's most famous club, The Wigan Casino, where Russ Winstanley began his all-nighters in late 1973.

*Opposite top inset:* Sew-on patch for 'Mr M's', the 'oldies' room which ran at The Wigan Casino

*Opposite bottom inset:* An early advert for the 6Ts club night at The Starlight Rooms in London, run by Ady Croasdell and Randy Cozens

*Top:* Keep the faith whatever you do: the classic Northern Soul logo

*Bottom:* Membership card for the 6Ts' all-nighters, which continue to run at The 100 Club on London's Oxford Street

Adidas sports bag adorned with patches from Northern Soul club nights, *circa* 1975

It was here that Northern Soul culture crystallised. Clothing was kept loose and baggy, with many kids bringing in a change of clothes in their holdalls. Stalls were set up around the venue to allow people to buy records. The DJs played rare vinyl discoveries, often covering up the record labels to ensure their exclusive rights to that particular song. Often only pressed in limited numbers by tiny record labels with names such as Wand, Swan and Golden World, these records are still highly collectable.

Within three years the club boasted a staggering membership of 100,000 and two years later it was voted the world's best disco. Yet the media spotlight the club attracted put off many of the hardcore, who moved onto pastures new. The Wigan Casino closed in 1981, although it is still fondly remembered by the thousands who spent many happy hours there.

In the 1980s a new generation of enthusiasts arrived. Ady Croasdell and Randy Cozens began a night which eventually settled at London's 100 Club under the name The 6Ts, where it has gained a reputation as one of the best Northern clubs in the country. Croasdell is also responsible for issuing a series of great compilations on the Kent Records label, which has breathed new life into songs such as 'Tainted Love' by Gloria Jones, Wigan standby 'Long After Tonight Is All Over' by Jimmy Radcliffe, 'No One to Love' by Pat Lewis, 'Do I Love You' by Frank Wilson, 'The Snake' by Al Wilson and 'Competition Ain't Nothing' by Little Carl Carlton, among many hundreds of others.

The Northern Soul scene has crossed over into the mainstream. You can hear its records on Radio 2 and on many TV adverts. Theatrical plays and films about the scene are also doing the rounds. As the badges always exhort us: Keep the Faith.

*Left:* 'Northern Super Soul' pin badge

*Right:* Sew-on patch celebrating three Northern Soul clubs: The Golden Torch in Stoke, The Twisted Wheel in Manchester and The Wigan Casino in, er, Wigan

# Online Modernism

In the last 15 years or so, the growth of the World Wide Web has been enormous. All kinds of information rest in cyberspace and Mod is no exception, with numerous blogs and websites providing up-to-date news on clothing ranges, bands, clubs, records and more. The website Modculture is regarded as the best of its kind in the UK. Its inventor, David Walker, started the site in 2000. His sole intention was to report on the Mod scene in the North of England. Interest from all over the UK persuaded Walker to expand the site. It reached a national audience by featuring reports and news on events around the country and further afield. The site also provides reviews and writings on all Mod-related subjects, from books to scooter rallies.

Walker's interest in the subject may be traced to his family. His older sisters attended The Wigan Casino and his brother was part of the late 1970s Mod revival. This close exposure to all

*Top:* Logo for Modculture.com

*Bottom:* Logos for The Modcast and Jack That Cat Was Clean

things Mod means that Walker retains a good knowledge of Mod culture in its widest sense. In its first year Modculture won a national web award and in 2011 it remains extremely popular, having embraced the social networks Twitter and Facebook.

Two other sites of great quality are Mod Generation (themodgeneration.co.uk), where Mods get together to swap stories and deliver fascinating articles on all kinds of subjects, and Jack That Cat Was Clean (jackthatcatwasclean.blogspot.com), a French initiative which posts great and rare TV clips as well as live footage of key Mod performers such as Georgie Fame and Junior Walker.

Over on Facebook and highly recommended is the 'Original Modernists 1959–1966' Facebook group, started by legendary clothes retailer Lloyd Johnson, which has over 2,000 members. A very active site which is widely read, plenty of rare photos pop up on it, with great discussions and music supplied by its members. Also worth checking is Eddie Piller's The Modcast (themodcast.co.uk), which has featured in the past such luminaries as Soho legend Mark Powell, Steve Cradock and Bradley Wiggins. As Pete Meaden might have exclaimed, 'Cyber-Modernism, it's the new thing, baby!'

# Ronan O'Rahilly

Magazine advert for Radio Caroline

It is easy to think of Ronan O'Rahilly as the Irish equivalent of Pete Meaden. He was a young man moving at a fevered pace, with ideas bubbling out constantly. But whereas the fragile Meaden failed in the rough and tough world of the music business, O'Rahilly proved to be a tougher proposition. He arrived in the UK in the early 1960s and before long was a familiar face on London's vibrant rhythm and blues nightclub scene. In 1964, aged just 23, he was running The Scene Club in Ham Yard, the club of choice for early Mods. O'Rahilly had also moved into management, co-managing the early Rolling Stones before taking on Alexis Korner and then Georgie Fame. Failing to get Fame a recording contract, O'Rahilly set up his own label, only to find he couldn't get any airplay for the resulting single. In the early to mid-1960s the BBC would only play records by established acts. Turning to the so-called 'independent' Radio Luxembourg,

Disc jockeys Robbie Dale (left) and Johnnie Walker, of ship-based pirate radio station Radio Caroline South, at Felixstowe after the British government outlawed the station under the Marine Broadcasting Offences Act, 14 August 1967. Despite the legislation, Radio Caroline continued broadcasting and was the only offshore station to defy the ban

Radio Caroline's pirate radio ship MV *Mi Amigo* runs aground at Frinton-on-Sea on the Essex coast during a storm, 20 January 1966

O'Rahilly was amazed to discover that the major labels of the day, EMI, Decca and Pye, effectively paid for their acts to appear on its airwaves. Again, it was a closed shop. It was then that O'Rahilly decided that if you can't beat them, join them. O'Rahilly bought a boat and docked it in his family's private port in Greenore, Ireland. The boat was then refitted as a radio station and christened the MV *Caroline*, named after President John F. Kennedy's daughter. On Easter Sunday 1964 O'Rahilly moored the boat just outside British territorial waters in Felixstowe, Suffolk, and Radio Caroline began broadcasting on the '199 Wavelength'. Disc jockeys who started at Caroline and who would go on to become household names include Tony Blackburn, Simon Dee, Johnnie Walker, Dave Lee Travis and Emperor Rosko. The effect of this new station on the youth of the UK was immediate and Caroline's adventurous playlists soon had listening figures of several million. The soul music that Mods adored could now be accessed on the airwaves. However, new government legislation passed by Tony Benn in 1967 outlawed the station. Over the intervening years O'Rahilly kept the station going and today it transmits from a land-based location.

O'Rahilly was executive producer on the film *Girl on a Motorcycle* (1968), which starred Marianne Faithfull, and he is also credited as being the person who talked actor George Lazenby out of signing up for a further seven James Bond films after Lazenby had taken the lead role in the film *On Her Majesty's Secret Service* (1969). O'Rahilly was convinced that the Bond movies wouldn't survive into the 1970s.

On Monday, 3 December 2007, Ronan O'Rahilly was inducted as a Fellow of the Radio Academy. Some might call this a great example of the condition known as extreme irony.

Ronan O'Rahilly, founder of offshore radio station Radio Caroline, in Dublin, early 1960s

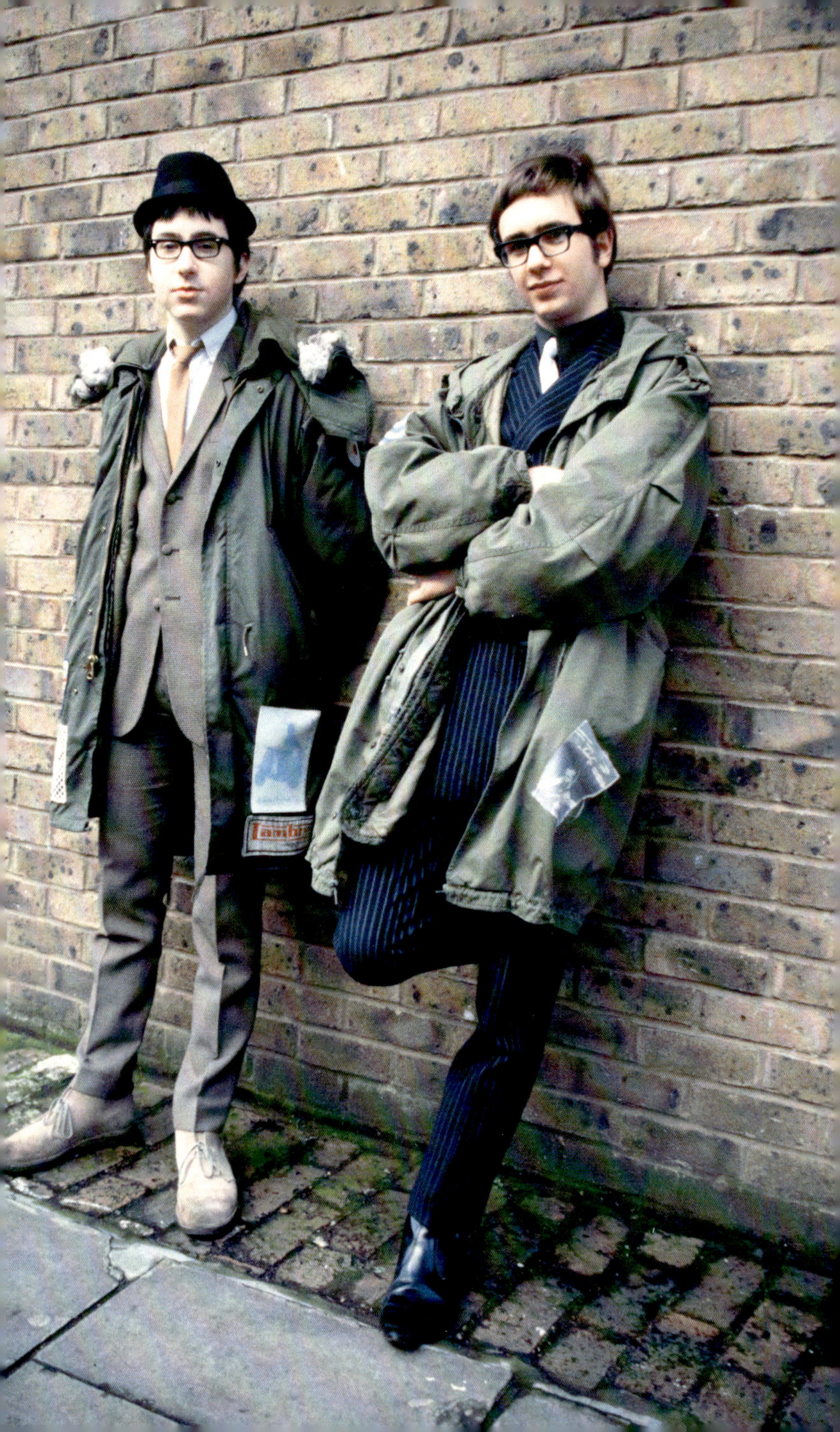

# The Parka

To the average man in the street, the parka is the one piece of clothing most associated with Mod. The word 'parka' comes from the language of the Nenet people of northern Russia, and loosely translates as 'animal skin'. The parka favoured by the original Mods was the American M-51 fishtail, which was introduced, as the name implies, in 1951. This coat first saw service in the Korean War. This is why the inner lining of the coat carried maps to be used by soldiers separated from their battalions. The 'fishtail' is the material at the back of the coat, which the wearer can wrap around his or her legs for further warmth and protection. The M-51 also had a removable fur-trimmed hood that provided extra windproofing.

The Korean War ended in 1953, but production of the M-51 continued until 1956. Stocks of the parka began turning up in the UK's many army surplus stores in the early 1960s

*Opposite:* Two Britpop Mods, London, *circa* 2001

*Top:* Even The Beatles loved a parka: John Lennon arrives at the EMI Studios in Abbey Road, winter 1966

*Top:* A Mod family shows its allegiance at the 1981 Loch Lomond Rock Festival in Scotland

*Opposite top:* Marines carry a wounded comrade through snow to a cleared airstrip for evacuation during the Korean War

*Opposite bottom:* Mods in Brighton, 1964

and were eventually picked up by Mods with scooters, for whom the coat was perfect. It was warm, kept the clothes underneath clean and doubled up as a sleeping bag if needed. Over the years, the original M-51 has become a very collectable item, fetching anywhere up to £1,000 for one in mint condition. There have been many variations and sub-standard parka copies made since they were first introduced and many purist Mods shun the parka as too inelegant. For the scooter rider or the Mod football fan, however, it remains the best protection against the elements.

195

# Peckham Rye

When it comes to scarves that boast great Mod appeal, an original Tootal is hard to beat (see Tootal Scarves). However, over the last couple of years a natural successor to Tootal's crown has been found. The company is called Peckham Rye, Cockney rhyming slang for a tie. It operates out of a small shop at 11 Newburgh Street, London W1, the very same street that Vince's Man Shop traded from in the late 1950s (see John Stephen). Peckham Rye can trace its roots back as far back as 1854, when one Charles McCarthy became a boy tailor in the British Army aged 14. Upon leaving the Army he set up business in the South London locale of Peckham. The present owner is the great-great-grandson of Charles, and he has followed his family heritage by applying exacting standards to Peckham Rye's products. This has resulted

# Peckham Rye
## LONDON

in the fine array of hand-made silk scarves, ties and handkerchiefs, made in paisley and polka dots and in vibrant hues, that can be found on their premises. With its close proximity to Carnaby Street, the Peckham Rye shop has been gathering a very healthy Mod following, exactly how they planned it. As the guys in the shop say, 'He who wears, wins ...'

*Opposite:* Photographer, filmmaker and DJ Dean Chalkley sports a Peckham Rye scarf, London, 2011

*Top left:* A classic blue and white spotted scarf

*Top right:* The Peckham Rye logo

*Bottom right:* Peckham Rye paisley tie

Mr Weller in his self-designed Fred Perry from 2006

# Fred Perry

If you have examined the wardrobe of any Mod over the past 40-odd years, we're pretty sure you will have found a Fred Perry polo shirt hanging there. The story of how it became a Mod fashion staple is one of the quirks of clothing history in the UK. The man himself, Frederick John Perry, was born in Stockport, Cheshire, in 1909. From 1934 to 1938 Perry was the number one tennis player in the world, both as an amateur and a professional. He won the Wimbledon Championship three times and became the first player ever to win all four Grand Slam titles. He also led a glamorous life off the court, which included a relationship with the actress Marlene Dietrich.

In the late 1940s, after retiring from tennis, he collaborated with the Austrian Tibby Wegner on the invention of the sweatband. Their next move was to design and produce a short-sleeved sports shirt, made from a white piqué fabric.

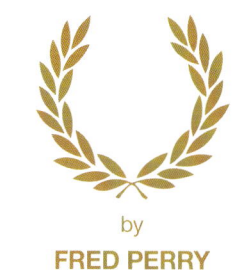

by
**FRED PERRY**

*Top:* The laurel-leaf logo

*Bottom:* A classic black Fred Perry polo shirt

**FRED PERRY SPORTSWEAR**

MEN'S WEAR CATALOGUE

FRED PERRY SPORTSWEAR LTD.
13 - 14, GOLDEN SQUARE,
LONDON, W.I.
Telephone: GERrard 5133 (5 Lines)

To give it a distinctive look, they added a laurel-leaf logo, embroidered on the left chest area. Unveiled at the Wimbledon tournament in 1952, it instantly became a bestseller.

The shirt began to be worn by Mods in the early 1960s. It was they who demanded that colours be added to the range to correspond with the colours of favoured football teams. The shirt was also popular with the original Skinhead movement that emerged in the late 1960s.

The shirt has never truly gone away but in the last five years the brand has re-emerged as a fashion leader, endorsed by the likes of Amy Winehouse and tennis player Andy Murray. A statue to Fred Perry was unveiled at the All England Tennis Club in 1984 and he died in February 1995.

In Manchester in the late 1970s a small cult calling themselves The Perry Boys emerged. Ian Brown and Mani from The Stone Roses were

*Top left:* The man himself: a very dapper-looking Mr Fred Perry

*Top right:* Fred Perry Men's Wear catalogue from the 1960s

*Bottom:* A 1950s polo shirt

# Fred Perry

**Big-wheel customers are looking for a look like this:** snappy roll-neck shirt in Bri-Nylon, with lace-knit front, plain back and sleeves. Great in white, gold or sage.

**Action customers are looking for a look like this:** lace-knit in Crimplene, with cut-away collar, short sleeves. Have it in store. In white, ice blue and oatmeal.

FRED◯PERRY   Fred Perry Sportswear Limited: 5 Vigo Street, London W.1. Sales Office: Bridport Road, London N.18.

among its practitioners. As their name suggests, they wore Fred Perry tops and followed bands such as The Jam. They died out quite soon but are fondly remembered by those in the know.

Company advertising from the 1960s

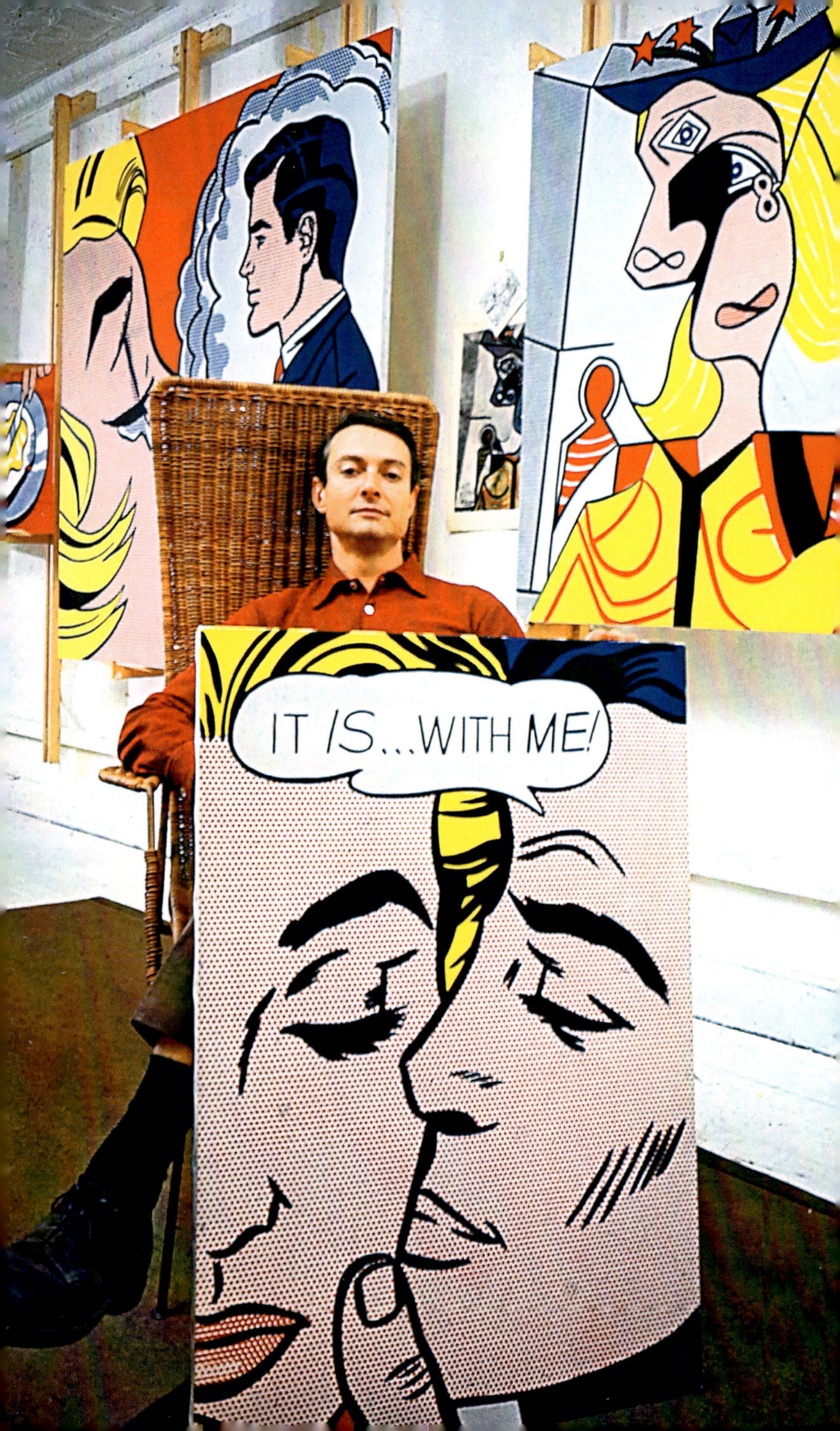
IT IS...WITH ME!

# Pop Art

Pop art is Keith Moon wearing a target tee-shirt, and Pete Townshend in a jacket made from an old Union Jack flag. Yet how many of the young fans of The Who realised they were looking at the influence of a major art movement? Pop art was a reaction to the dominant Abstract Expressionist movement of the time. It used everyday objects and cultural references in an ironic way, poking fun at 'high art' and its 'intellectualisation'. The Scottish artist Eduardo Paolozzi started it in the UK with his collage *I was a Rich Man's Plaything* (1947), which included the first use of the word 'pop' in a work of art. Peter Blake's collage *On the Balcony* soon followed, while in America the artist Jasper Johns produced *Flag* (1954–5), although its impact was not really felt in the US until the late 1950s.

In the UK Blake's impact was to inspire artists of the calibre of Pauline Boty, Bridget Riley, Brian Rice and Richard Hamilton, who created work

*Opposite:* Artist Roy Lichtenstein holding one of his creations in 1963

*Top:* British Pop artist Pauline Boty at home with her cat, *circa* 1963

British Pop artist Sir Peter Blake standing in his garden in Chiswick, 1963

that still resonates to this day. Blake himself went on to design the famous *Sgt Pepper's Lonely Hearts Club Band* album cover for The Beatles in 1967 and Hamilton landed its follow-up, creating the famous all-white sleeve for the band's ninth album, *The Beatles*. In the US Andy Warhol with his famous *Campbell's Soup Cans* and the DC comic book-style paintings of Roy Lichtenstein were very influential, the lettering section of Lichtenstein's *Whaam!* (1963) ending up on a Paul Weller Rickenbacker guitar. Later on, Weller completed the circle by asking Blake to design the cover for his bestselling *Stanley Road* album of 1995.

Other major practitioners of Pop art were The Creation (see The Creation) and The Who (see The Who), specifically on their second album, *A Quick One* (1966), whose genesis was forged from Pop art methods. On the album the (inspired) music is interrupted by radio adverts and announcements while the sleeve is designed in Pop art style. For art student Pete Townshend, Pop art, with its emphasis on the everyday, was perfect for aligning with his songs.

In recent times Ed Ball, the Mod underground musician, has consistently incorporated Pop art into his oeuvre. He has started a label called Whaaam Records, used Pop art styles on his album covers and adopted a Pop art approach to his songwriting by penning songs with titles such as 'We Love Malcolm' and 'I Helped Patrick McGoohan Escape'. For one of his albums Ball handpainted every cover individually.

Given the immediacy of both Pop art and pop music, it is surprising how rarely they have merged.

British artist Brian Rice with some of his work, 1964

# *Quadrophenia* – The Film

For many late 1970s Mods the film *Quadrophenia* was essential. As far as they could see, the film had everything – the music, the clothes, the scooters and the lovely Leslie Ash. *Quadrophenia* is a classic teen movie, although for some its lack of attention to detail is at odds with the true Mod ethos.

*Quadrophenia* is based on the 1973 album of the same name by The Who. Its 1979 release chimed perfectly with the Mod revival. The film follows the day-to-day existence of a 1965 Mod called James Michael Cooper, played brilliantly by actor Phil Daniels, although he nearly failed to get the part which would launch his career. The film's director, first-timer Franc Roddam, had screen-tested Sex Pistols front-man John Lydon for the part, but insurance problems meant that Daniels got the job. After shooting began, the film was placed in jeopardy when The Who's legendary drummer Keith Moon

*Opposite:* Alleyway coming up! Garry Cooper as 'Pete' and Leslie Ash as 'Steph' in a scene from the film

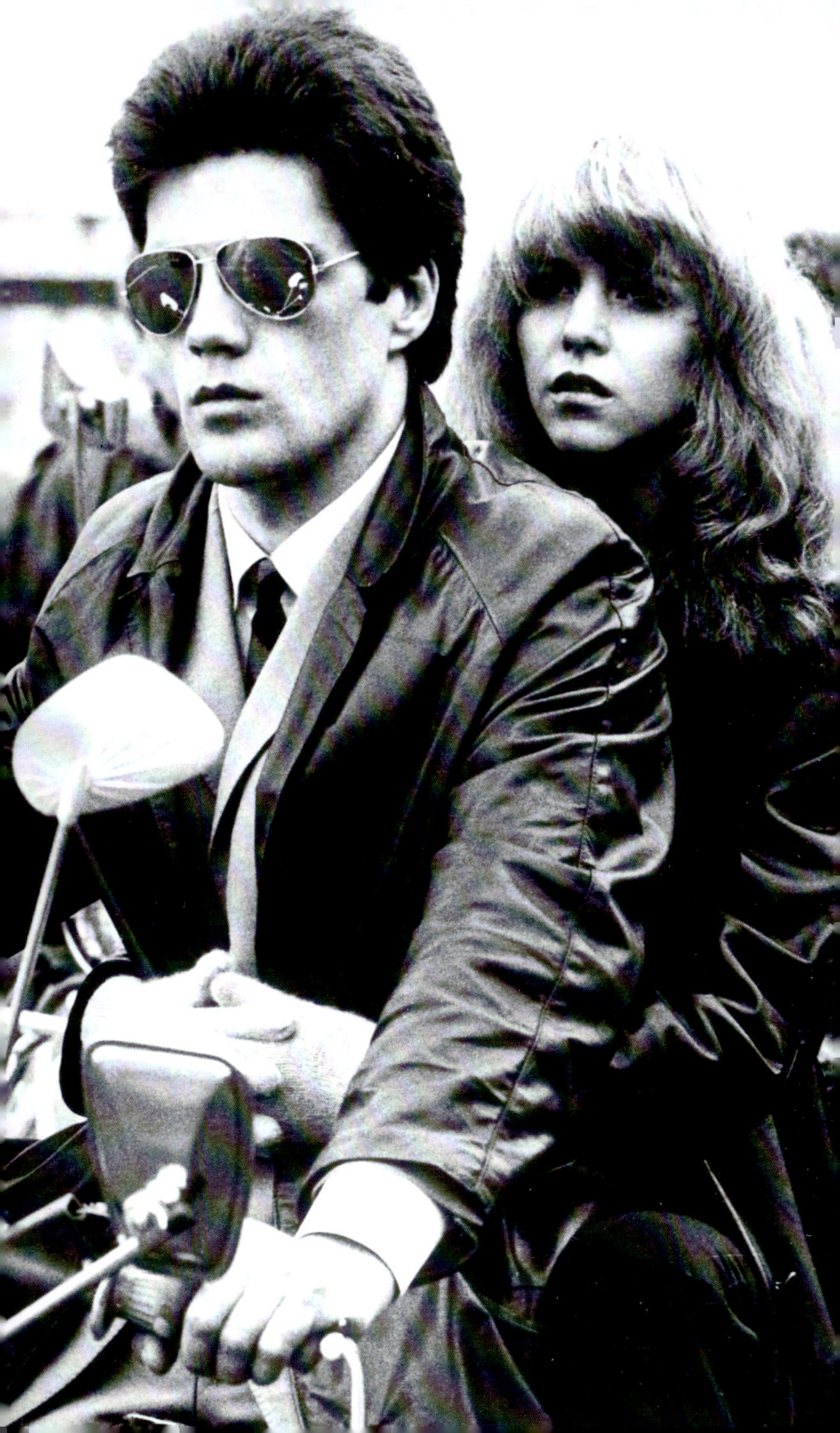

Leslie Ash with Phil Daniels as 'Jimmy' on Brighton Beach

died, but the production ploughed on. The film follows Jimmy living the life of a Shepherd's Bush Mod, riding his scooter around town, falling out with his parents, getting fitted for suits, having his hair cut and trying his hardest to chat up Steph, the love of his life. His bedroom walls are covered in newspaper cuttings of beach fights between Mods and Rockers and photographs of The Who's Pete Townshend. Eventually, events conspire to render Jimmy suicidal and he is last seen riding a stolen scooter along the coastal clifftops of Beachy Head in Sussex. The scooter is then seen flying over a cliff and the viewer is left to figure out our hero's fate.

Unfortunately, the film contains many incorrect details and for Mod purists has no value whatsoever. As a classic teenage film, though, it stands the test of time and is fondly regarded by many. The famous child dancer and 1960s DJ Jeff Dexter was the choreographer in charge of getting Sting to dance. Also notable in the film are the number of young actors who went on to carve careers for themselves in the worlds of TV, film and music: step forward Ray Winstone, Sting, Phil Daniels, Phil Davis, Toyah, Mark Wingett, Leslie Ash, Michael Elphick, Timothy Spall, Gary Holton, John Altman and John Bindon, among others.

Front cover of The Who's album *Quadrophenia* (1973)

# Mary Quant

As every good student knows, the 1960s began in the 1950s. Mary Quant is a classic example of this theory. Although now mostly associated with 1960s fashion, Mary opened up her first shop, Bazaar, at 138A King's Road, Chelsea, in 1955. Bazaar is now cited as the first-ever boutique. If male Mods had Carnaby Street, then Mod girls had Quant.

Quant was born in Blackheath in 1934. While studying at the nearby Goldsmiths College she met Alexander Plunket Greene. Together they hatched plans to open a clothes shop specifically aimed at the young. The pair – who would later marry – were joined in their venture by money man Archie McNair. Once opened, Bazaar became famous for its colourful and often daring window displays and quickly became a focal point for the so-called 'Chelsea set', which included the models, photographers and pop stars of the day, as well as young aristocrats looking for fun.

A model wearing a mini-dress in bonded wool jersey, inspired by a football strip, designed by Mary Quant's Ginger Group

Mary Quant peers over the top of a copy of French *Vogue*, featuring Twiggy on the cover, sitting in her London boutique in 1967

Mary Quant's shop, Bazaar, on the King's Road, Chelsea, London, 25 August 1966

As the shop prospered, the world began to take notice of the designs Quant was producing. Within seven years the business was worth over £1 million and her clothes were available worldwide. Along with fellow designers André Courrèges and John Bates, Quant is now credited with inventing the miniskirt. She would later argue that it was the girls of the King's Road who actually invented the skirt, and that she had just adapted their ideas commercially.

Quant's own style was similarly groundbreaking. Vidal Sassoon created a bob haircut for her, which instantly marked her out from her contemporaries. Quant also produced accessories and make-up ranges, which all sported her distinctive signature black-and-white daisy logo. In 1966 she was awarded the OBE for services to the British fashion industry, and in the late 1960s she again displayed her great talent for innovation by introducing hot pants to the market.

Alexander Plunket Greene died in 1990, and in 2000 the business was sold to a Japanese group. Now in her seventies, Quant lives quietly in the English countryside and gives the occasional lecture to fashion-hungry students.

A small cloth-covered case, watch and talcum powder by Mary Quant

R

# Ready, Steady, Go!

'The weekend starts here!' And it most certainly did. Following on from previous TV pop shows such as *Six-Five Special* and *Oh Boy!,* in August 1963 Associated Rediffusion launched their new flagship show, *Ready, Steady, Go!,* which was broadcast live from Studio Nine in Kingsway, London, at 6 p.m. every Friday. It quickly became a must-see for London's teenagers. Later on, when it was broadcast nationally, it made Mod a nationwide youth cult and thus – unknowingly – hastened its decline.

The show was the idea of Elkan Allen, then head of Rediffusion TV. The original theme tune for the show was 'Wipe Out' by The Surfaris, but was later changed to '5-4-3-2-1' by Manfred Mann. The show was presented by the solid, dependable Radio Luxembourg DJ Keith Fordyce, and the often scatty but 'with-it' Cathy McGowan (see Cathy McGowan). A younger male presenter, Patrick Kerr, was added later on.

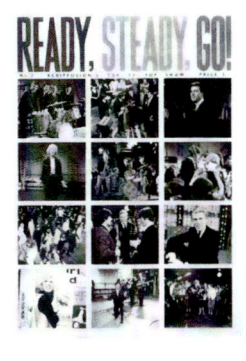

*Opposite:* The singer Millie performing at the *Ready, Steady, Go!* studios in Kingsway, London

*Top:* Cover of *Ready, Steady, Go!* magazine

The highly fashionable teenage audience was handpicked from Mod clubs and thus looked great and danced beautifully. But it was the acts that appeared on the show that the viewers really tuned in for. The Beatles, The Rolling Stones, Dusty Springfield, James Brown, The Who, Georgie Fame, The Beach Boys, Marvin Gaye, The Kinks, Otis Redding, Cilla Black, The Small Faces and The Walker Brothers were just some of the acts featured. The often chaotic scenes in the compact studio only added to the general excitement of the show.

*Left:* The Yardbirds perform on *RSG!* Drummer Jim McCarty, guitarist Chris Dreja, bassist Paul Samwell-Smith, singer Keith Relf and soon to be guitar god Jeff Beck, March 1966

*Right:* Owner of the *RSG!* video archive, Dave Clark, drummer – surprisingly enough – of The Dave Clark Five, seen here in 1964

Eventually the show moved to a later time slot and a larger studio in Wembley, with McGowan now the sole presenter. By 1965 all the bands featured were performing live on the show. However, by then the BBC had started *Top of the Pops* which, with its up-to-date chart listing, soon began to attract more viewers. Although still very successful, *Ready, Steady, Go!* was eventually cancelled in December 1966, but it has gained a huge cult status as the years have rolled by. In 1983 a production company owned by former pop star Dave Clark released a compilation video of various performances from the show, which immediately topped the sales charts. Other volumes followed, including the Otis Redding and Motown specials. Keith Fordyce died in 2010, aged 83.

Motown legends The Four Tops perform the hit single 'Standing in the Shadows of Love' on the programme

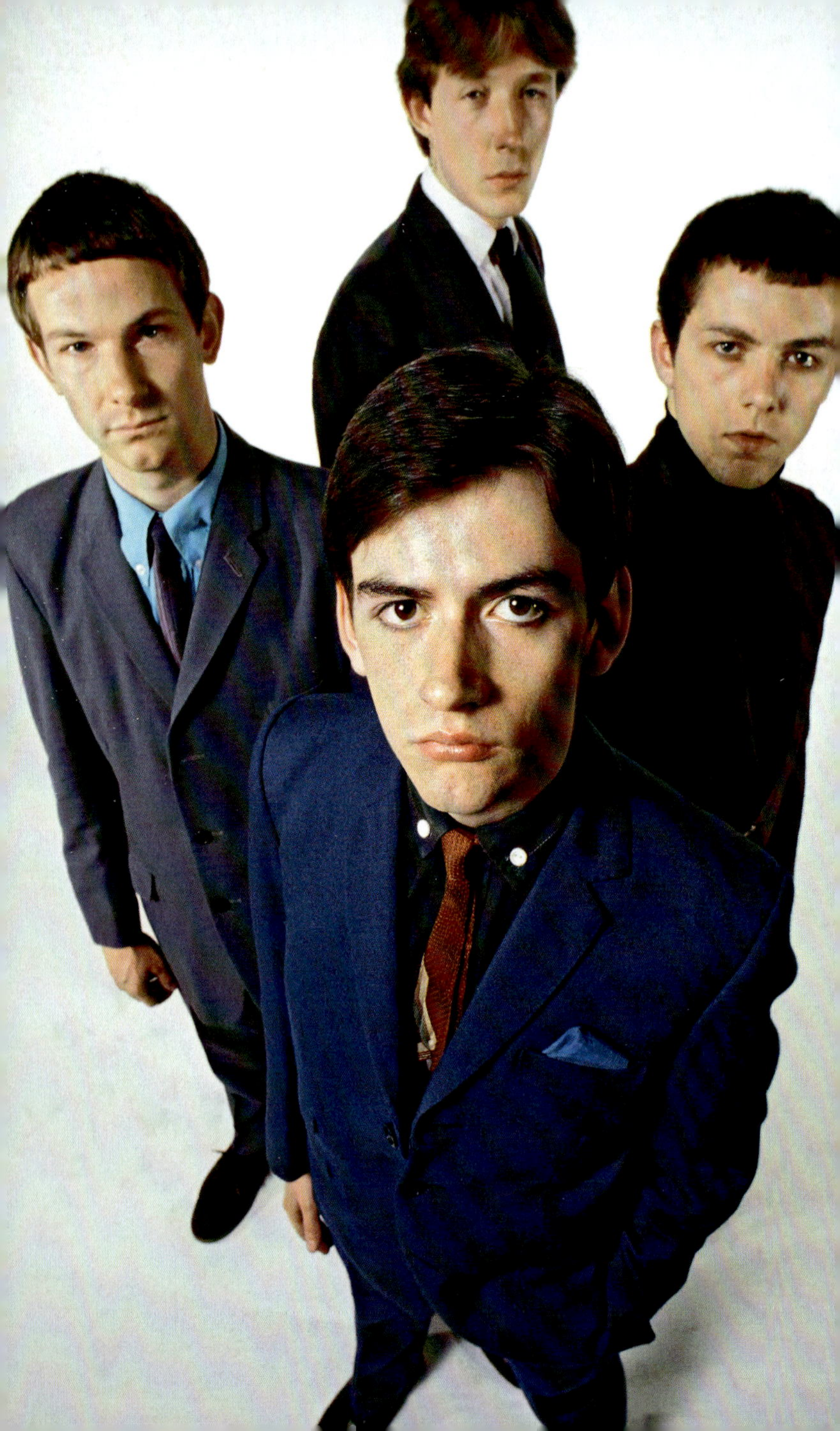

# Revival

The Mod revival of 1979 – sparked by the film *Quadrophenia* and the startling success of The Jam – gave us a number of bands that are still fondly remembered by that generation. Top of that particular list would have to be Secret Affair, who shone very brightly for a couple of years. Formed in 1979 by vocalist Ian Page and guitarist Dave Cairns, both of whom had played in the band New Hearts when they were just 16, and with Seb Shelton on drums, Dennis Smith on bass and Dave Winthrop on saxophone, Secret Affair attained both single and album chart success very quickly. As was the fashion at the time, the band were quick to start their own label, I-Spy Records, through an agreement with Arista. Their debut single, the anthemic 'Time for Action', was released not long after, reaching number 13 in the charts and selling over 200,000 copies. It was followed by 'Let Your Heart Dance', which again went top 40. Page by this time was

*Opposite:* Secret Affair, 1979. From the top clockwise: Dennis Smith, Dave Cairns, Ian Page, Seb Shelton

*Top:* A flyer for the re-formed Chords' Glasgow show, 2010

Millions like us: Jeff Shadbolt, Gary Sparks, Simon Stebbing and Bob Manton of The Purple Hearts before their 100 Club in 2009

all over the music media and was quickly dubbed the 'spokesman of a generation' for his forthright views on a range of topics. Some loved him, many loathed him, but you couldn't escape him.

In December 1979 the band released their debut album, *Glory Boys* (the name given to their followers), which peaked at number 41 in the charts. A better placing was achieved the following year for their single 'My World', although 'Sound of Confusion', its follow-up, and their new album, *Behind Closed Doors* (1980), failed to dent the top 40. By now the whole Mod revival movement was beginning to run out of steam, a fact recognised by Seb Shelton, who left to join Dexys Midnight Runners. He was replaced by Paul Bultitude. After a long tour of the USA the singles 'Do You Know' and 'Lost In the Night' along with the album *Business as Usual* (1982) were released, but none of them were successful and the band split in 1982.

Cairns continues to work in the USA, and Page releases some solo material, but the glory days are gone. The band joined forces again 20 years later and have continued to tour sporadically ever since. They have found an audience revelling in the memories of a band they still love.

Another band that have re-formed lately are The Purple Hearts. Evolving from a Romford-based punk band called The Sockets, vocalist Bob Manton, guitarist Simon Stebbing, drummer Gary Sparks and bassist Jeff Shadbolt formed this band in 1978. Taking their name from the popular Mod drug, they signed to Fiction Records and released their popular single, 'Millions Like Us', which got to number 57 in the pop charts in 1979. They proved a popular live band, touring with the likes of Secret Affair and winning over a lot of audiences. Their debut album, *Beat That* (1980), was produced by Jam producer Chris Parry and 'Jimmy', the single from it, reached number 60.

And the way they were...
The Hearts, *circa* 1980

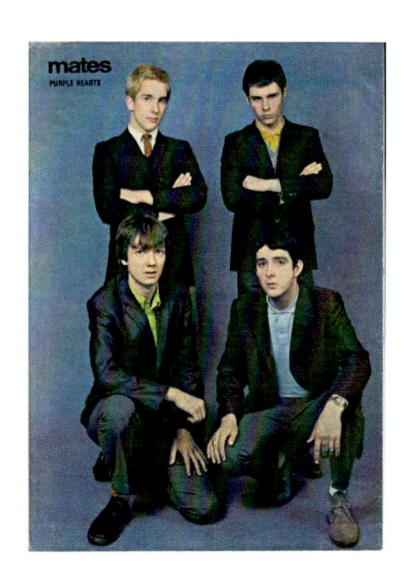

The band split in 1982 and all the members went their separate ways. After a couple of short-lived reunions in the intervening years, The Purple Hearts re-formed in 2009, playing sell-out gigs all over the UK, including a rousing night at The 100 Club on Oxford Street in London. Always fondly remembered by the now fortysomething Mod enthusiast, the Hearts were an inspiration to many. Acid Jazz head honcho Eddie Piller, when a fledgling Mod, named his fanzine *Extraordinary Sensations* after one of the band's B-sides. It is also worth noting that this scene provided a great platform for top DJs such as Paul Hallam and Mod scribe Terry Rawlings.

The other most popular band to emerge from the Mod revival scene of the late 1970s were The Chords. The band began in south-east London in 1978. Vocalist Billy Hassett was joined by Martin Mason on bass, Brett 'Buddy' Ascott on drums and Chris Pope on guitars and main songwriting

The Purple Hearts in *Mates* magazine, *circa* 1980

duties. The band hit the gig circuit, recorded a session for John Peel and were featured on the cover of *Time Out*. They also supported The Undertones, The Jam and Secret Affair. They signed to the Polydor label and although their first single, 'Now It's Gone', failed to sell, its follow-up, 'Maybe Tomorrow', hit the top 40 in January 1980. An album, *So Far Away*, was released in May 1980. Constant touring followed but further chart success was not to be and, following a few more single releases, the band fell apart in 1981. The original band re-formed in 2010 and toured the UK to promote their single 'Another Thing Coming'.

By 1982 the Mod revival was finished, and eyes were looking elsewhere.

The Chords, *circa* 1979.
L to R: Chris Pope, Brett 'Buddy' Ascott, Billy Hassett, Martin Mason

# Rickenbacker Guitars

For two of the Mod world's leading lights, the shape and style of their guitar is often as important as their clothes. In the case of Pete Townshend and Paul Weller, Rickenbacker guitars have been their number one choice on several occasions. 'I chose a Rickenbacker simply because The Beatles were using them', said Townshend in 1964. Townsend used a 360/12 on the seminal recordings of 'I Can't Explain' and 'Anyway, Anyhow, Anywhere' and a model 1998 on the 'My Generation' recording and regularly during 1965 and 1966. This is also the guitar featured on the famous 'Maximum R'n'B Marquee' poster that is so synonymous with the band. Pete was as well known then for smashing the guitars to pieces while on stage as he was for actually playing them. And they didn't come cheap. An imported one at that time would set you back about £169, a large amount of money then.

*Opposite:* Pete Townshend windmilling away at his Rickenbacker, 1966

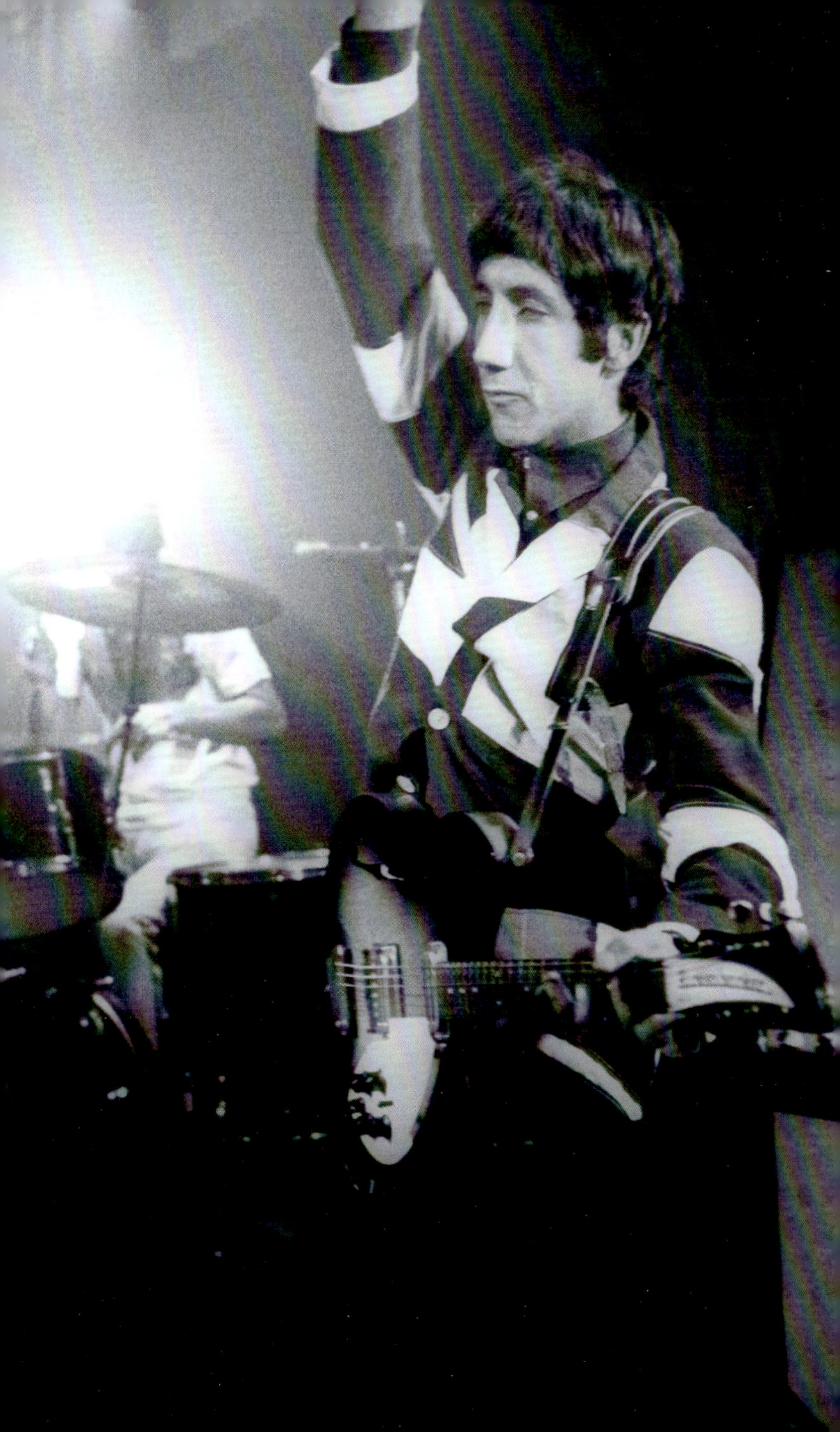

*Top:* John of the Fab Four seen here with his 'Rick' on the TV show *Thank Your Lucky Stars*, 1964

*Opposite top:* Paul Weller of The Jam backstage after a gig surrounded by Rickenbackers, *circa* 1978

*Opposite bottom:* A 1958 Rickenbacker 425

Fast forward to 1978–9 and Paul Weller is explaining his guitar choice when starting life in The Jam. 'The first attraction was the look, because I liked Pete Townshend on the early Who stuff. When I got an advance from the record company I went out and bought as many Rickenbackers as I could.'

The distinctive name comes from company founder Adolph Rickenbacker, a Swiss émigré who, along with George Beauchamp, formed the company in Los Angeles in 1931. Rickenbacker specialised in steel guitars until the advent of the rock'n'roll boom of the 1950s, when they turned their focus onto standard acoustic and electric guitars, introducing the Capri Series in 1958. John Lennon bought a 325 Capri while in Hamburg in 1960 and continued using a 'Rick' (as they were nicknamed) throughout the early stages of Beatlemania, including the band's groundbreaking appearance on *The Ed Sullivan*

*Show* in February 1964. During that same tour of the USA, George Harrison began using a twelve-string Rickenbacker, model 360/12.

Other well known 'Rick' players include Roger McGuinn of The Byrds, Carl Wilson of The Beach Boys, John Entwistle of The Who, Fred Smith of The MC5, Bruce Foxton of The Jam, Andy Bell of Oasis and Beady Eye, Noel Gallagher, and Sergio Pizzorno of Kasabian.

# The Roundel

*Top:* An alternative roundel pin badge

*Bottom:* A scooter parked on Southend seafront in 2007 with a roundel design on the spare wheel cover

*Opposite top left:* Women pilots of the Air Transport Auxiliary (ATA) adjusting their parachutes, *circa* 1943. Note the RAF roundel painted on the fuselage of the aircraft behind them

The David Wedgbury photograph of drummer Keith Moon wearing a tee-shirt with a large red, white and blue 'target' on its front has become one of the most iconic Mod images. The target – or the roundel, to give it its proper name – came to prominence when Peter Blake used it in his painting *The First Real Target* (1961). It then began to pop up in several Pop art images. The Mods later adopted it as their badge of honour.

The disc-shaped roundel can be dated back to the twelfth century, when it appeared in various colours on the many coats of arms which were unique to a person or a family. The French Air Force later displayed a roundel on its aircraft during the First World War. Using the colours of their national flag as inspiration, this roundel had a large red ring outside a white circle with a dark blue centre. Many other air forces designed their own roundels, with the Royal Air Force reversing the red and blue rings to form the 'target' we know so well today. Look on any high street and you'll still see it used on all types of clothing and collectables. It has become a design classic.

*Top right:* Targeting the smoker: anti-smoking advert from a mid-1960s *Rave* magazine

*Bottom left:* Newspaper advert for military jackets with a nod to the Keith Moon 'target tee'

*Bottom right:* The clothing company Ben Sherman have long used the roundel as part of their advertising campaigns

S

# The Scooter

Launched at a Roman golf club in April 1946, the scooter revolutionised travel in Italy and went on to establish itself as Mod's greatest symbol. Thanks to media coverage of the bank holiday riots of 1964 and 1965, the Mod and the scooter are now inextricably linked.

The Vespa and the Lambretta were products of the Second World War, the conflict that shattered Italy's economy. Cheap transport was now desperately required for workers. Enrico DiMaggio was a former aircraft maker whose factory had been badly hit by Allied bombs. He was approached by an engineer named Corradino D'Ascanio, who had just fallen out with another industrialist named Fernando Innocenti. Like Piaggio, Innocenti had been keenly aware of Italy's need for cheap transport and had worked with D'Ascanio on a prototype based on the Cushman scooter issued by the US army. After they parted ways D'Ascanio

*Opposite:* Mod Michael Pain climbing aboard his scooter on Carnaby Street, July 1964

*Top:* Vespa pin badge

*Bottom:* Lambretta advert, *circa* 1955

approached Piaggio, who employed him straight away. D'Ascanio's great innovation was to place the engine at the back of the vehicle, causing Piaggio to exclaim, 'It looks like a wasp!' *Vespa* is the Italian word for wasp. A year later, Innocenti launched the Model A Lambretta scooter, named after the river Lambro, which ran near his factory in Milan.

Both scooters were very popular with the impoverished Italian public. They were affordable, functional and very stylish and both companies made fortunes. By the late 1950s – thanks to recovering economies and a new sense of freedom transmitted through films such as *Roman Holiday* (1953) – the scooter became a new symbol of liberation. In London Vespas and Lambrettas began to appear and, like their Italian counterparts, Mods quickly took to them. Scooters gave them mobility and allowed the driver to remain smart and clean while buzzing

*Top:* A group of Mods and their scooters outside a labour exchange in Peckham, South London, 1964

*Middle:* Lambretta pin badge

*Bottom:* The classic Vespa 125

around town, which one could never achieve on a larger motorcycle. With hire-purchase payment plans now available, a parka-clad Mod heading for the seaside became a familiar sight and sound.

As the motor car became readily affordable, sales of scooters declined all over Europe. In 1972 Lambretta was taken over by the Indian government and its dominance faded. Vespa suffered too but has kept going. Back in the UK, however, the magic of this stylish vehicle persists, with scooter clubs all over the country attracting thousands to sold-out rallies.

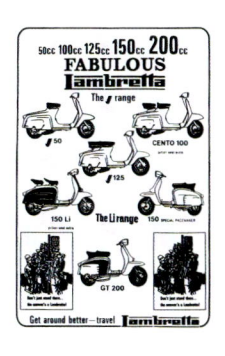

*Top:* Scooter? – Check. Parka? – Check. Let's go! A young Mod about to ride off on his beloved machine

*Bottom:* Trade advert for Lambretta scooters

# Ben Sherman

The man who shot to fame as Ben Sherman was born Arthur Benjamin Sugarman in Brighton in 1925. After emigrating to the USA in 1946, Sugarman married into the family of a Los Angeles shirt manufacturer and began working for the family business. However, he soon became disenchanted with the company's conservatism and, on returning to the UK in 1963, began designing his own range of American-style shirts in bright, pastel colours and vibrant stripes. He called the shirt after himself and it soon became an instant hit with the Mod fraternity. By 1966 Sherman had moved to Carnaby Street and by 1969 the company was selling thousands of shirts a week. The Mod's spiritual brothers, the Skinhead and the Suedehead, were big supporters of the Ben Sherman shirt.

In the early 1970s, taking advantage of favourable British tax laws, Sherman moved to

Ben Sherman plectrum logo

Derry, Northern Ireland, where it is said Catholics and Protestants never once attacked his factory; Ben Sherman crossed all divides.

Today 1960 originals fetch a tidy price on the vintage circuit and there is a flagship Ben Sherman shop on London's Carnaby Street as well as a bespoke suit store at 39 Savile Row. Sherman himself died in 1987.

*Top:* Shirts, shirts, everywhere... The interior of the Ben Sherman flagship store in New York

*Bottom left:* The man himself (right) with his sales director Ronnie Wiseman on a trip to New York in 1969

*Bottom right:* Marcus Sherman modelling a shirt from the boys' range in 1969. We all wanted one!

**235**

Album cover of the *Small Faces* LP for Decca Records, 1966

# The Small Faces

For many The Small Faces were the ultimate Mod group, and that is because – crucially – they were Mods who formed a band, not the other way around. Therefore they always got it right, whether in the studio or in front of a camera. They were the same height (five foot five) and of the same mentality, and their bond was rock-hard until fame and time withered it away.

Formed in 1965 with one-time child actor Steve Marriott up front on lead vocals and guitar, Ronnie 'Plonk' Lane on bass, Kenney Jones on drums and Jimmy Winston, later replaced by Ian 'Mac' McLagan, on keyboards, the band worshipped rhythm and blues greats like Otis Redding, James Brown, Bobby Bland and Inez and Charlie Foxx. The term 'blue-eyed soul' could have been invented for Marriott. His voice was a thing of true wonder and acted as a source of inspiration for countless performers, including Led Zeppelin's Robert Plant.

Pin badge inspired by the cover of the 1968 *Ogdens' Nut Gone Flake* album

The perfect pop group
at the *Ready, Steady, Go!*
Wembley studios, 1966.
L to R: Ian McLagan, Ronnie
'Plonk' Lane, Kenney Jones,
Steve Marriott

From their early days, Steve and Ronnie wrote their own material, and after the usual round of gigs in pubs and small venues, they got a residency at The Cavern Club in London's Leicester Square, where the London Mod scene quickly latched onto them. Their raw retelling of blues and r'n'b songs won much favour with discerning Modernists. A real buzz about the band was created and before long they had signed a deal with manager Don Arden, who placed them with Decca Records. Arden was a clever operator. He saw what the band's Achilles heel was and milked it endlessly. He gave them a house in Pimlico and a Rolls-Royce but, more importantly, he gave them accounts in nearly every clothing shop on Carnaby Street. When it came to dishing out the royalties, Arden would point to their clothes bills as the reason why they were in effect penniless. The band did not care. As long as they looked the business and had a pound in their pocket, then all was well in the world. They became true fashion leaders, their innate Mod style beautifully transmitted in every shot taken of the band. Today, these pictures still sparkle with colour and inventiveness.

After two years of success and fighting with Arden and Decca, the band were picked up by the new Immediate label, run by former Rolling Stones manager Andrew Loog Oldham. By this time the band had discovered LSD and the drug served to change not only their music – which became very psychedelic – but also their look. The hair grew longer and the clothes became more colourful and way-out. Yet the band still

All too beautiful: Marriott, McLagan, Jones and Lane looking every inch the Mod gods they were in early 1966 looked great. They were in effect creating a trailblazing Mod/hippy look, neatly bringing together two opposing fashions. Musically, The Small Faces flourished on Immediate, producing a string of fantastic singles – 'Here Come the Nice', 'Tin Soldier', 'Lazy Sunday' – and two highly regarded albums, *Small Faces* (1967) and *Ogdens' Nut Gone Flake* (1968), which came with an innovative round album sleeve designed to resemble an old tobacco tin.

After the relative failure of the single 'The Universal', Marriott quit the band on New Year's Eve 1968, and went on to form Humble Pie with Peter Frampton. Jones, McLagan and Lane teamed up with Rod Stewart and Ronnie Wood to create The Faces. Ronnie later went solo and had success with the songs 'How Come' and 'The Poacher', among others. The Small Faces reunited briefly in the mid-1970s, but Lane soon left. Sadly, Marriott died in a fire at his home

The original band line-up with Jimmy Winston (far left) in 1965 in Essex in 1991 aged just 44, and Ronnie Lane succumbed to multiple sclerosis in 1997. Jones went on to tour as the replacement for Keith Moon in The Who, and McLagan has recorded under his own name, as well alongside The Rolling Stones and Billy Bragg.

Interest in the The Small Faces peaked again in the Britpop era (see Britpop) of the mid-1990s, with the likes of Paul Weller and Noel Gallagher citing the band as a major influence. A City of Westminster plaque commemorating the band was unveiled in 2007 on their former stomping ground of Carnaby Street. The 15th annual Small Faces Convention took place in London in 2011 and was attended by a thousand devotees from all over the world.

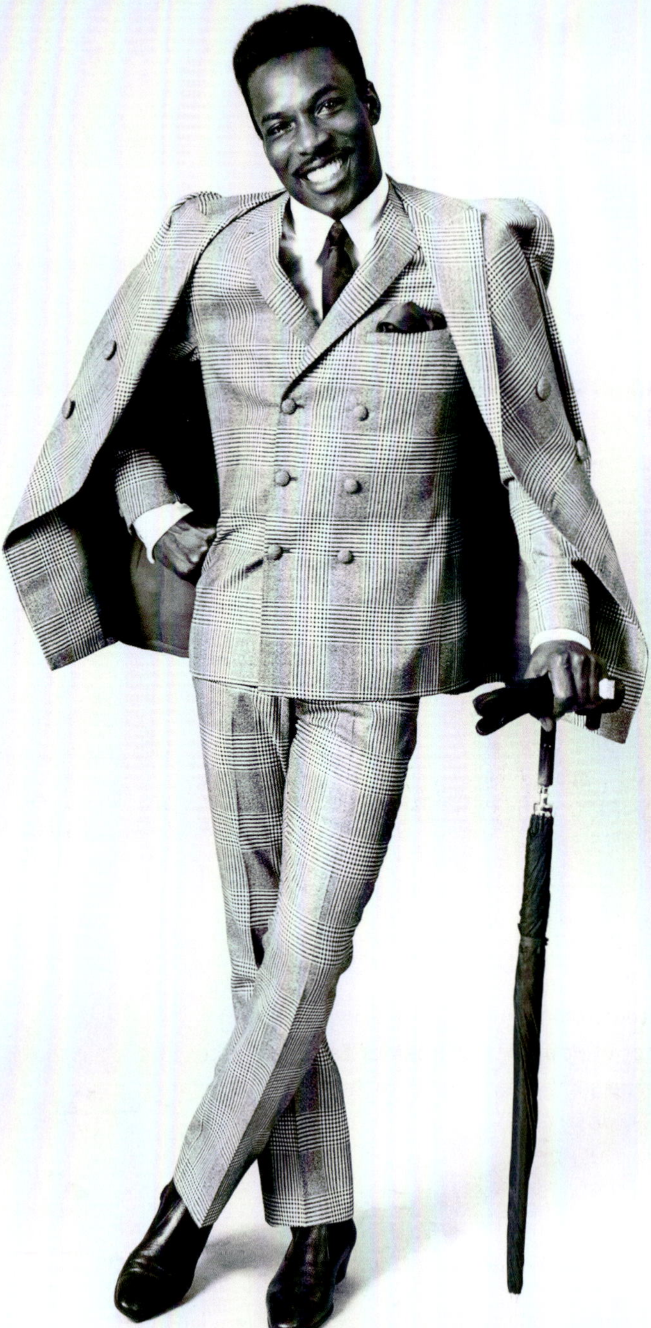

# Stax Records

The finger-snap logo of the Stax record label is as instantly recognisable as the sweet music that was recorded for it. It all began in 1957 when bank worker and part-time fiddle player Jim Stewart began recording local country and western acts in his garage studio, based in Brunswick, Tennessee. He then released the records on his own small Satellite record label. Stewart wanted to upgrade his recording equipment and asked his elder sister Estelle Axton for a loan. She agreed but asked to join his operation. Together they bought an Amplex 350 tape recorder. The siblings moved to Memphis in 1960, and began working out of an old movie theatre at 926 East McLemore Avenue, south Memphis.

Estelle ran the Satellite Record Shop at the front of the building, selling a variety of records by different labels to generate extra income while Jim ran the studio. That summer they recorded 'Cause I Love You' by local disc jockey Rufus

*Opposite:* Never mind the Prince of Wales, here's the Prince of Soul. Wilson 'The Wicked' Pickett wears it well in 1963

*Top:* The unmistakable finger-snap logo of Stax

Founders of the label Jim Stewart and his sister Estelle Axton in the mid-1960s

Thomas and his daughter Carla. Atlantic Records vice-president Jerry Wexler became aware of this regional hit, and optioned future releases in a five-year deal. Carla's follow-up, written by her father, was called 'Gee Whiz (Look At His Eyes)' and went top five nationally. Having noted another record label called Satellite operating out in California, Stewart decided on a name change. Taking the first two letters from his surname and the last two letters from Estelle's, he came up with Stax.

A local piano player, Booker T. Jones, was soon hanging around the studio and he soon teamed up with guitarist Steve Cropper, bass player Duck

Dunn and drummer Al Jackson to form Booker T and the MGs (the last standing for Memphis Group). Used alongside 'The Memphis Horns' as backing on many of the label's classic recordings, the group produced one of the first and finest Mod classics in 'Green Onions' in September 1962. Cropper went on to co-write many songs and act as house producer for Stax.

In 1962, at a Johnny Jenkins recording session for Atlantic, work was finished half an hour earlier than expected. Otis Redding, a member of the band, seized the chance to record a song he had written called 'These Arms of Mine'. The song was a local hit and Otis went on to become one of soul music's greatest stars, a true Mod hero with his impassioned delivery, innate good nature and wonderful mohair suits.

By this time, Atlantic Records was sending down its own performers to record at Stax. These included Sam and Dave, and Wilson Pickett, who

Al Bell, Vice President of Stax Records, sits in his office in Memphis, Tennessee, 1960s

The label of the 7" single 'I Thank You' by Sam and Dave, 1968

joined up with recent Stax signings such as Eddie Floyd and William Bell. Also present was the talented songwriting duo and production team Isaac Hayes and David Porter. Among the songs they wrote for Sam and Dave were the Mod classics 'Hold On I'm Coming' and 'Soul Man'. Many made comparisons with Berry Gordy's Motown but Stax always delivered a much rougher, rawer sound than their counterparts in Detroit.

In 1965 Jim Stewart hired Al Bell, a successful DJ, to take over the day-to-day running of the company. Estelle left, citing differences with Bell. In December 1967 Stax was shaken to its foundations when Otis Redding and some members of The Bar-Kays died in a plane crash after a hugely successful European tour and groundbreaking appearance at The Monterey Pop Festival. His next release, '(Sittin' On) the Dock of the Bay', became his biggest seller.

The initial deal Wexler had agreed with Stewart in 1962 was coming to an end. During the renegotiations, it was discovered that the original contract had given Atlantic ownership of all the Stax master tapes. Stewart ignored the option of re-signing with Atlantic and instead sold the company to Gulf and Western for millions of dollars. Despite these events, Stax continued to have hits with Booker T and the MGs and William Bell.

In 1969 Isaac Hayes put aside his producing ambitions and came into his own when his album *Hot Buttered Soul* went triple platinum. He then recorded perhaps his most famous album, the soundtrack to the blaxploitation film *Shaft* (1971), which made him a worldwide star. Meanwhile, internal strife caused by the Gulf and Western deal forced Jim Stewart and Al Bell to buy back the company. After a period of readjustment, the hits began to flow again and Stax entered a second golden period. The Staple Singers, Jean Knight and Mel and Tim led the way with chart hits. Buoyed by their success, in August 1972 Stax presented the 'Wattstax' event, a festival of black acts, which later became known as the 'Black Woodstock'. The event drew a crowd of over 100,000. In the same year, Al Bell made a deal with Columbia Records to distribute his releases in an attempt to compete with Motown Records. Bell used the money he earned to buy out Stewart.

By 1973 the deal with Columbia had gone sour and Stax was in serious financial trouble. Its last real chart success of note was 'Woman to Woman' (1974) by Shirley Brown. In a vain attempt to rescue the company, Jim Stewart came back once again, but it was too late. Sadly, he ended up losing all of his money. Unable to honour its payroll and declared bankrupt, Stax closed on January 1976.

By 1977 virtually all of the Stax assets had been bought by Fantasy Records of San Francisco. The Stax Museum of American Soul Music opened on the old site in 2003, and contains thousands of pieces of memorabilia from the label's heyday. Stax remains a quintessential Mod label.

The frontage of Stax Records, early 1970s

# John Stephen

From a very early age John Stephen had had one ambition driving him forward. 'If my work means a young man can walk down the street in a pink shirt one day and not be called a queer, then I will have succeeded.' Stephen realised his dream and did so in an impressively short time.

Born in 1934, and raised in the tough area of Govan in Glasgow, Stephen first trained as a welder before the attraction of London became too strong to resist. He landed there in 1952, worked as a waiter and then moved to the clothes retailer Moss Bros. From there he found a dream job working for Bill Green in a shop called Vince on Newburgh Street, literally around the corner from a dowdy cut-through which in a few short years would become world-famous as Carnaby Street. Vince sold flamboyant and often daring clothes to a 'theatrical and artistic' customer base. Jazz singer and writer George Melly once famously said of the shop

*Top:* 'Carnaby St. Mods' pin badge

*Opposite:* Street sign for John Stephen on Carnaby Street, early 1980s

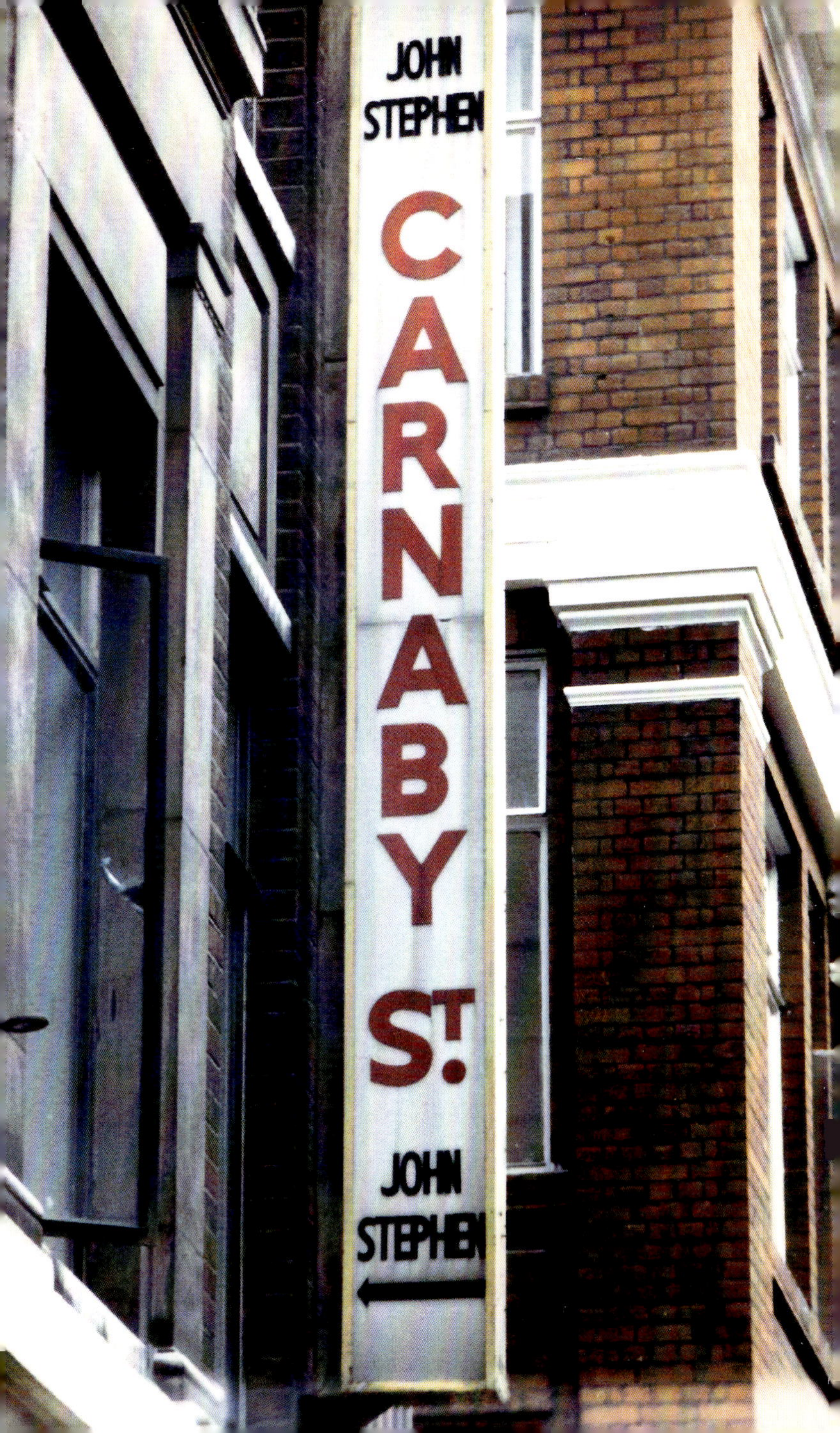
JOHN
STEPHEN
CARNABY
ST.
JOHN
STEPHEN

Frontage for the Male W1 shop, *circa* 1966

that 'It was the only place where they measured your leg when you bought a tie.'

Stephen always had a nose for fashion. He was the first to import Levi's jeans in the UK, a venture so successful that he was able to buy his first Rolls-Royce by the age of 20. Encouraged by his success, Stephen began to manufacture his own designs, many made in colourful and patterned fabrics. He opened up his first shop, His Clothes, on Soho's Beak Street in 1957. His stock of hipster trousers in bright colours, tab-collared shirts and matelot sweaters sold very well. However, a small fire put paid to the unit in Beak Street, and after licking his wounds he re-opened at 5 Carnaby Street. It was the beginning of a beautiful journey.

Stephen aimed directly at the youth market. The shop's exterior was painted bright yellow. Window displays were explosions of colour and imagination, instantly catching the eye of the male teenager with disposable money burning a hole in his pockets. Pop music blared out from the shop, another first. Soon Stephen's business was prospering and the fast turnover approach he developed proved a forerunner to the likes of Topshop today.

Stephen and his partner, Bill Franks, began opening more shops on Carnaby Street. They gave them names such as Domino Male, Lord John and Male W1. Such was the hoopla surrounding his business that Stephen was soon supplying the pop stars of the day with clothes for their TV performances. Clients included The Beatles, The Small Faces, The Who and The Rolling Stones. Garments worn by these pop gods would instantly sell out. The media loved him, dubbing him the '£1m Mod' and 'King of Carnaby Street'.

Stephen himself was a conservative dresser, always in an immaculate bespoke suit and white shirt. He bought a succession of Rolls-Royces and

Always a man of many talents, John Stephen takes an order over the telephone while sorting a suit for a customer in-store, 1966

was accompanied everywhere by his German Shepherd dog, Prince. Through it all he retained the Glaswegian inflection to his speaking voice, by now sprinkled by a touch of the London Cockney. By 1967 he had 15 shops on Carnaby Street alone, others dotted around London and franchises in the USA and Russia. He was also the first within fashion to associate himself with football; the 'John Stephen' pitchside advertising banners appeared in Mexico during the 1970 World Cup.

Carnaby Street had become world-famous but had been of little interest to purist Mods for years. They viewed its popularity with great distaste and mistrust. By 1970 its heyday was over, and Stephen, with his sharp business sense, had moved on. He moved into wholesale and opened a factory back in Glasgow. He sold the John Stephen name and began importing high-end European fashions for the Francisco-M chain. He also acquired the franchises for several companies, including Lanvin. The John Stephen archive was later acquired by the Victoria and Albert Museum in London.

Dogged by ill-health, he retired in 2002, and he died in February 2004 aged 69. In 2005 Westminster Council unveiled a plaque to John Stephen on Carnaby Street in recognition of his contribution to fashion in the UK. The ceremony was attended by his long-time partner Bill Franks. The year 2010 saw the publication of an in-depth biography of him by Jeremy Reed, titled *The King of Carnaby Street*.

Strike a pose! John Stephen (second right) with three models wearing his designs on Carnaby Street, 1966

# Stone Foundation

Stone Foundation are a seven-piece band inspired in part by Mod and soul music and great clothes. The group – Neil Sheasby (bass), Neil Jones (vocals), Nikki Sandal (guitar), Ian Arnold (keyboard), Phil Ford (drums), Spencer Hague (trombone) and Lynn Thompson (trumpet) – emerged from the Midlands after years of hard practice and began to deliver support performances which often usurped the night's headline acts. For many, the band's power and style recall the early Dexys and, like them, Stone Foundation understand the importance of appearance, often taking to the stage in colourful Gabicci-style tops, waistcoats, suits, shirts, ties and collarless shirts. They have cut two albums and just released a Best Of compilation (*Three Shades of Stone Foundation*), which is marked by the band's musical inventiveness and talent. By bringing over vocalists such as Nolan Porter ('Keep On

*Top:* Logo from a Stone Foundation tee-shirt

*Opposite top:* The band in the rehearsal space. L to R: Nikki Sandall, Phil Ford, Lynn Thompson, Spencer Hague, Neil 'Sheas' Sheasby, Ian Arnold with (front) Neil Jones

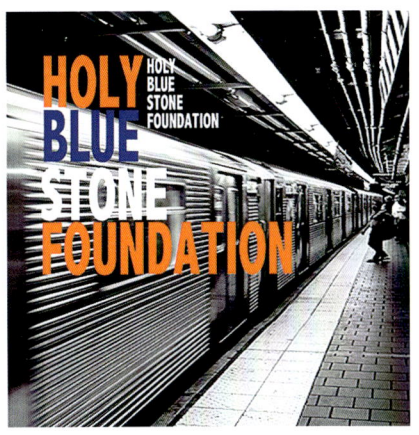

Keeping On') and Joe Harris ('The Undisputed Truth') to work with them on their own brand of deep soul and Mod pop, Stone Foundation have made clear their intent: to be a band to keep your Modernist sunglasses fixed on.

*Bottom left:* Three shades of the Stone Foundation: Sheas, Jonesy and Nikki from the band

*Bottom right:* Cover of the single 'Holy Blue', 2011

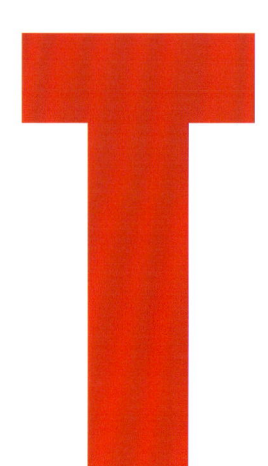

# James Taylor Quartet

Spinning off from the remnants of their previous Kent-based band The Prisoners, James Taylor and Allan Crockford formed the James Taylor Quartet in 1986. Making overt their interest in all things cinematic and Mod, they released a version of the Herbie Hancock tune 'Blow Up' on the Re-elect the President label, an early forerunner of Acid Jazz Records. John Peel picked up on the tune and an album followed in 1987, titled *Mission Impossible*. This work featured Hammond organ-flavoured covers of 'Mrs Robinson' and 'Alfie', among others. Championed by the neo-Mod scene of the time, the band became firm favourites on the live circuit. Signing to Polydor, they released the albums *Wait a Minute* (1988) and *Get Organized* (1989). Their single for the offshoot Urban label, 'The Theme from *Starsky and Hutch*', is perhaps their best known song, along with 'Austin's Theme' from the *Austin Powers* films. In the early 1990s they were joined by vocalist Noel McKoy for the single 'Love the Life' and their subsequent album *Supernatural Feeling* (1991), both of which charted. They turned full circle by re-signing with Acid Jazz Records for the release of their next album, *In the Hand of the Inevitable* (1995). In recent years the band have concentrated on touring, clocking up thousands of gigs around the globe, and have developed the Hammond organ sound to showcase a more funky style. James Taylor has also recorded incidental music for television shows and the Quartet have since recorded as the New Jersey Kings.

*Top left:* The sleeve for *The Money Spyder*, 1987

*Top right:* James Taylor tinkles the ivories

*Bottom:* The record sleeve for *Mission Impossible*, also from 1987

# Tootal Scarves

The Modernist's number one scarf is made by the Tootal company. Tootal's ability to create imaginative paisley and polka-dot designs have drawn thousands of Mods to their creations and put the company way ahead of its competitors. In keeping with their Mod heritage, Tootal are also one of England's oldest brands. The business was founded in Manchester by textile merchant Robert Gardner in 1799. In 1842 the Tootal family took over and by 1888 had registered the name Tootal Broadhurst Lee Co Ltd. After the First World War their scarves proved quite popular among the working class, but it was during the Second World War that they became a fashion accessory, when RAF pilots took to wearing them on a daily basis. As a result of this alliance, the scarves – as well as the RAF logo – were adopted by the 1960s Mod brotherhood. Thanks to the likes of Paul Weller, Oasis and Ocean Colour Scene the scarf was given a new lease of life in the mid-1990s and its popularity continues to this day. It is a vital component of the total Mod look.

*Top and bottom left:* Highly collectable vintage Tootal scarves

*Bottom right:* Company advertising for Tootal ties

Perfecto! Twiggy wearing a fashionable yellow-collared outfit with a multi-coloured floral kipper tie, 1968

# Twiggy

Another to be nicknamed the Queen of Mods, Twiggy can lay claim to being one of the first supermodels. A young British girl, like Jean Shrimpton just before her, she took the London look around the world. Twiggy's boyish hairstyle and androgynous features echoed a certain Mod sensibility while her dress sense reflected the aspirations of many young Mod girls. Her impact in America was such that it helped – along with The Beatles – to create Mod in America.

Twiggy was born Lesley Hornby in North London and at 16, after her photo was spotted in the Mayfair hairdressers Leonard, she was acclaimed the face of 1966 by the *Daily Express*. Fame quickly enveloped her but her down-to-earth nature – she never could see what the fuss was about, and told the world exactly that – boyish looks and sharp dress sense created her strong connection to a large audience of working-class girls. Her tendency to be shot in

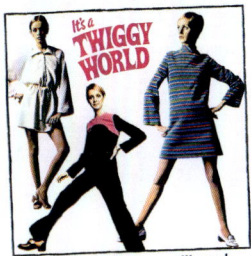

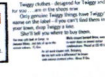

It's a Twiggy world, we just live in it: pages from late 1960s Freemans mail-order catalogues featuring the clothing range designed and modelled by Twiggy

street Mod fashions gave her the Queen of Mods title. When Mod passed out of fashion, Twiggy was in America posing for *Vogue* and was about to successfully enter the world of film. To this day she remains a British icon.

*Top:* Twiggy modelling a shirt from her own collection, May 1967

*Opposite:* The face of 1966. Beautiful, just beautiful...

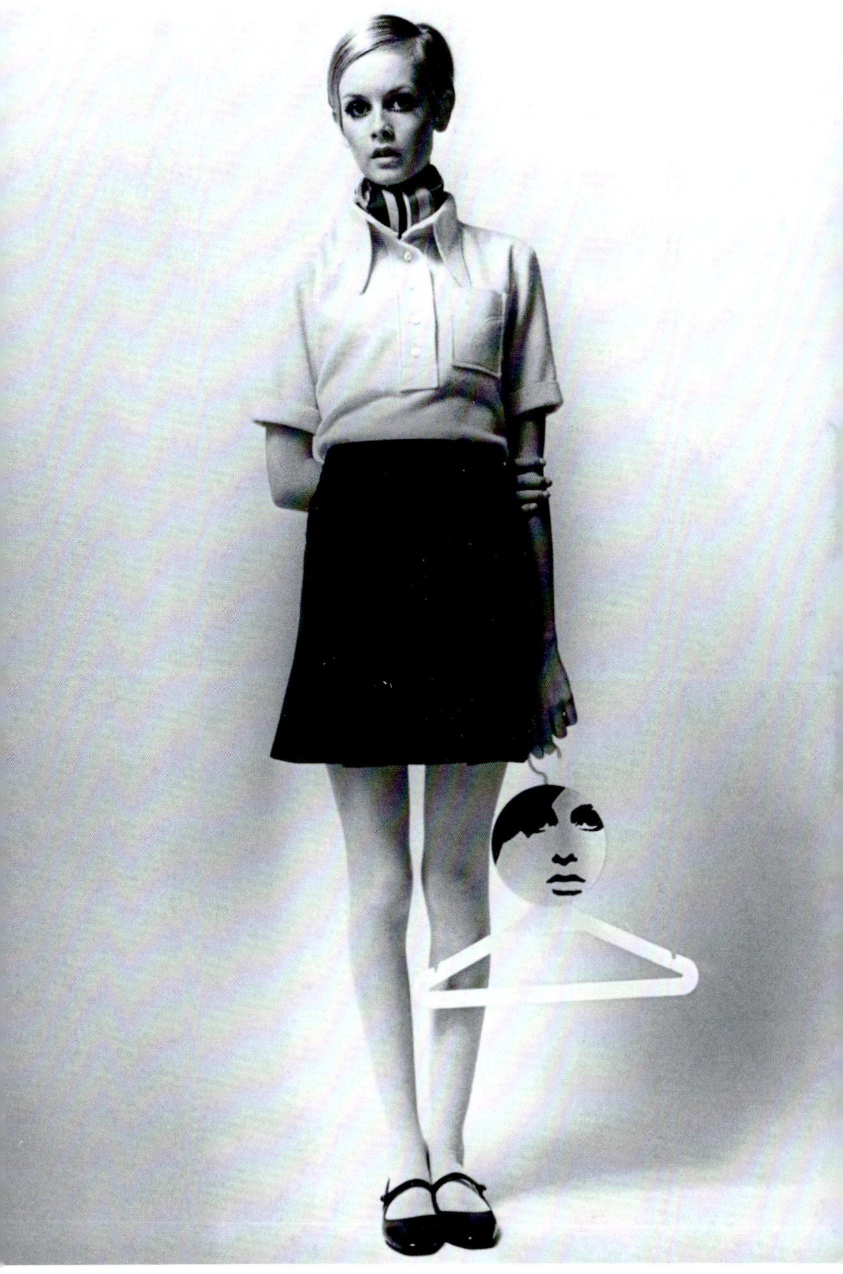

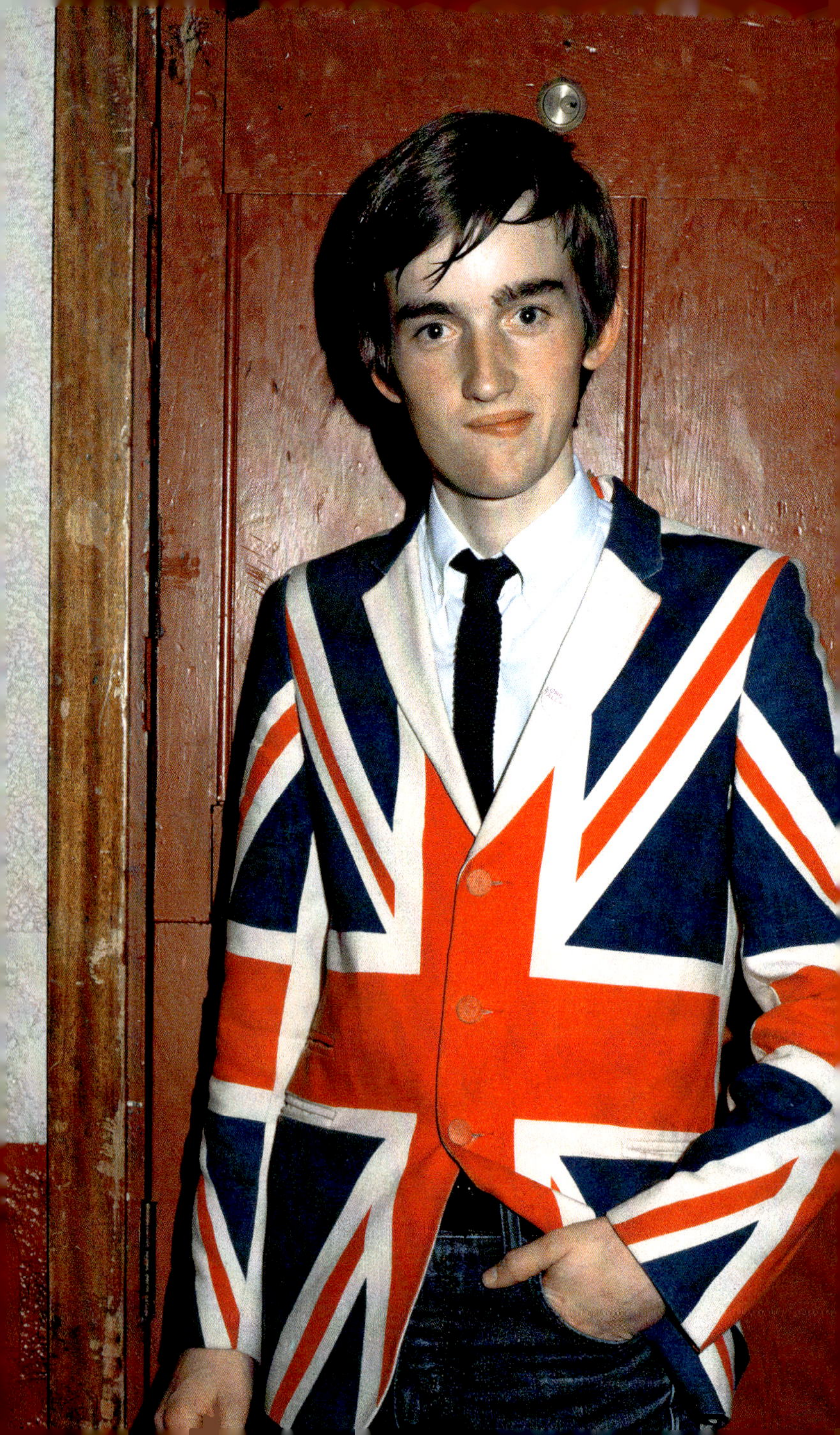

# The Union Jack

The use of the Union Jack in clothing began when Pete Townshend of The Who hit upon the radical idea of having the flag tailored into a jacket. The band first approached Savile Row tailors, who haughtily declined to have anything to do with defacing the national flag. Their second port of call was the East End, where tailors instantly asked, 'How many do you want?' In a stroke, Townshend had created a garment that has gone down in the annals of Mod history. His aim was to rebrand the flag as a piece of 'art'. A photograph of The Who, with Townshend in his coat by Colin Jones, made the front cover of an *Observer Magazine* in March 1966.

The current design for the 'Union Flag' dates from 1801 and comprises the crosses of St Patrick of Ireland, St Andrew of Scotland and St George of England. The word 'Jack' was in common use as an alternative to the word 'flag' and was often used by the Admiralty, who in

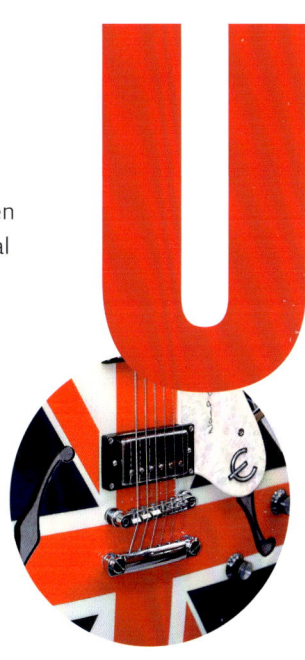

*Opposite:* A young Mod wearing a Union Jack jacket, *circa* 1980

*Top:* An Epiphone guitar owned by Noel Gallagher complete with Union Jack paintwork

267

The 'Best of British' window display on Carnaby Street, 1968

1902 decreed that 'Union Jack' was to be the flag's official name henceforth.

Fast forward to the late 1970s and the three members of The Jam admired Townshend's idea so much that they each had similar jackets made for a set of promotional photos taken in 1977. In his Jam days, Paul Weller often had a Union Jack draped over his guitar amps at gigs, again a Townshend initiative, with the words 'Fire and Skill' written on it.

The Gallagher brothers from Manchester's Oasis were never ones to let a good idea pass them by. Early artwork advertising the band's concerts showed a Union Jack being flushed down a toilet to celebrate their huge success. Noel Gallagher's girlfriend, Meg Mathews, handed him an Epiphone Sheraton guitar that had been given a Union Jack paint job, which he subsequently used frequently on the 'What's the Story  Morning Glory' tour. Liam had his clothing company, Pretty Green, make him a one-off Union Jack parka for the Isle of Wight festival appearance of his new group Beady Eye in June 2011, and one wall of the Pretty Green shop on Carnaby Street is dominated by a picture of him wrapped in the flag. A case of 'I'm all right Jack', some might say …

Pop art as clothing: Pete Townshend in the original jacket, performing with The Who in 1966

# Justin de Villeneuve

Justin de Villeneuve remains a classic example of the early Modernist mindset. This is a man who changed his name to suit his occupation, who ran with villains, boxed, cut hair and launched one of Britain's first ever supermodels, whom he also dated for many years. He was a working-class boy who desired riches, clothes and women and got all of them in huge quantities.

Nigel Jonathan Davies was born in the East End of London. As a child during the Second World War, he was evacuated to the Hertfordshire home of the great writer J. B. Priestley, an experience that he always said played a huge part in shaping his character for the better. As a young man he worked as a doorman for the famed Mod club La Discotheque, owned by landlord Peter Rachman. Thanks to his other 'underground' activities, Davies could often be seen down on Savile Row, ordering bespoke suit after suit. To be able to shop on the Row as a working-class boy was some achievement in those times.

Davies then found work as a hairdresser and changed his name to Christian de Forget. This led to a meeting with Twiggy and another change of name, as Justin de Villeneuve became her agent and her lover. The two eventually fell out. By that time, De Villeneuve had taken to photography. He later published a wonderful memoir – *An Affectionate Punch* – in which his own street slang is scattered liberally throughout the pages. He now lives on the coast with his wife, the designer Sue Timney. He photographs birds, stands up when women enter the room and still looks great.

*Left:* Twiggy with Justin, then her manager and boyfriend, 1968

*Right:* Book jacket for De Villeneuve's autobiography, *An Affectionate Punch*, published in 1986

THE PAUL WELLER
MOVEMENT

PAUL
The Jam

1977-1982
JAM

WELLER
LIVE!
plus special guests
LONDON
ALEXANDRA PALACE
MONDAY 5 DECEMBER
Doors open 6.00pm
www.paulweller.com
£30
8093

# Paul Weller

It is of course no secret that all aspects of the world of Mod have deeply influenced Paul Weller throughout his lengthy career as a musician. Mod music, clothes, books and films and the Mod mind set have inspired the songwriter from day one. One could say that Mod is in the fabric of his soul. 'It's like a religion. It's my code, it gives something to my life, I'm still a Mod, I'll always be a Mod, you can bury me a Mod', he told TV host Jonathan Ross in 1991.

John William Weller was born in Woking, Surrey, in May 1958. He was unofficially re-named Paul by his family while still a baby. He came from a solid working-class background, with his dad, John, working as a minicab driver and builder and his mum, Ann, a cleaner. A sister, Nicky, was born five years later. During his formative years, Weller discovered the twin loves that have remained constant in his life: music and clothes. His first musical love was

*Opposite top:* Cover of the single 'Into Tomorrow' by The Paul Weller Movement, released in 1991

*Opposite bottom:* A collection of Weller memorabilia

The Jam on stage during a live concert at The Top Tank, Reading, June 1977

The Beatles and by the age of 11 he had also developed a passion for clothes, following all the trends of the day. Musically, his career has been divided into three distinct phases: The Jam, The Style Council and his current solo adventure.

The Jam drew upon 1960s Mod as their main source of inspiration. This was the Mod of Carnaby Street and Union Jack jackets, scooters and bouffant haircuts, Pop art influences and Mod psychedelia. This was the Mod of the council estate and above all the Mod of The Who and The Small Faces, two bands who would play a crucial part in developing Weller's music and look. Weller first heard The Who in 1975 and along with Doctor Feelgood used The Who's early aggression and energy to push forward his band. As he would later admit, The Jam's first album was basically a musical rewriting of The Who's. However, as sales declined, Weller was smart enough to know he could not carry on nicking 'Pictures of Lily' riffs all his life. He now developed The Jam's own sound though key albums such as *All Mod Cons* (1978), *Setting Sons* (1979) and *Sound Affects* (1980). His ability to create a Mod music of the present that drew on the past brought him a huge, mostly male teenage audience.

Yet Weller could never rest on his laurels. In the early 1980s he was heavily drawn back towards the soul music of his youth, especially acts such as Chairmen of the Board or labels such as Invictus. He also fell badly for The Small Faces, whose ability to create an authentic mix of pop and soul Weller sought to emulate. In fact, such was his enthusiasm for Steve Marriott's 1960s wardrobe that when Marriott was asked if he liked Weller, he replied, 'Of course I do. He looks just like me.'

By 1982 Weller had had enough of The Jam. The three-piece line-up of the band was too restrictive and he yearned for a challenge to upset the predictability of his career. His Modernism had helped ring the changes. The catalyst was the Colin MacInnes book *Absolute Beginners* (see *Absolute Beginners*), which explored the roots of Modernism, the world of coffee bars and cool jazz. With his new band, The Style Council, Weller joined this world with a pro-European attitude and his clothing now expanded to take on colourful jumpers, Ray-Ban sunglasses, cut-off Levi's, smart blazers (*à la* the Modern Jazz Quartet), Burberry raincoats, white Levi's, French hairstyles and loafers. The use of Tonik suits was a nod to his Suedehead days while drummer Steve White exerted a distinct casual influence on the band's look. Weller's extensive knowledge of clothes and styles, coupled with his creative nature, allowed him to set the pace for many years in the late 1980s.

*Opposite:* Foxton, Buckler and Weller, March 1978

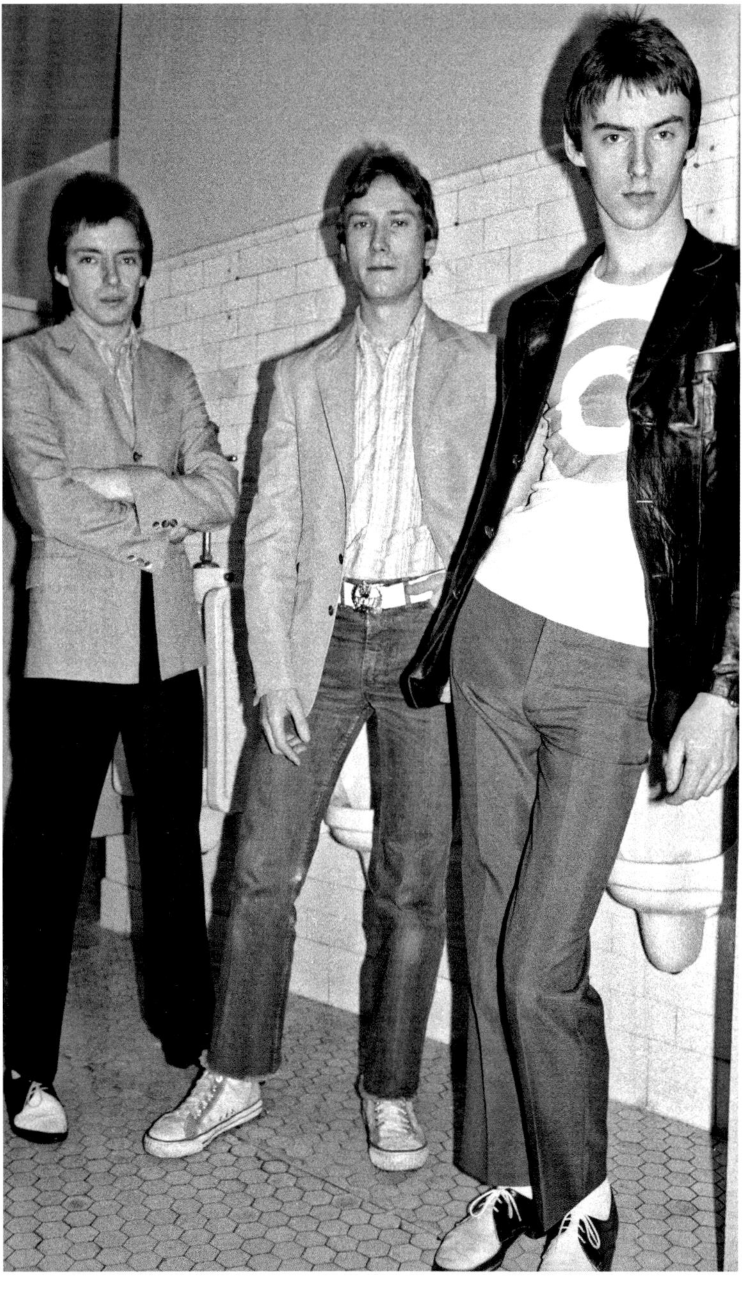

The *À Paris* EP by The Style Council, 1983

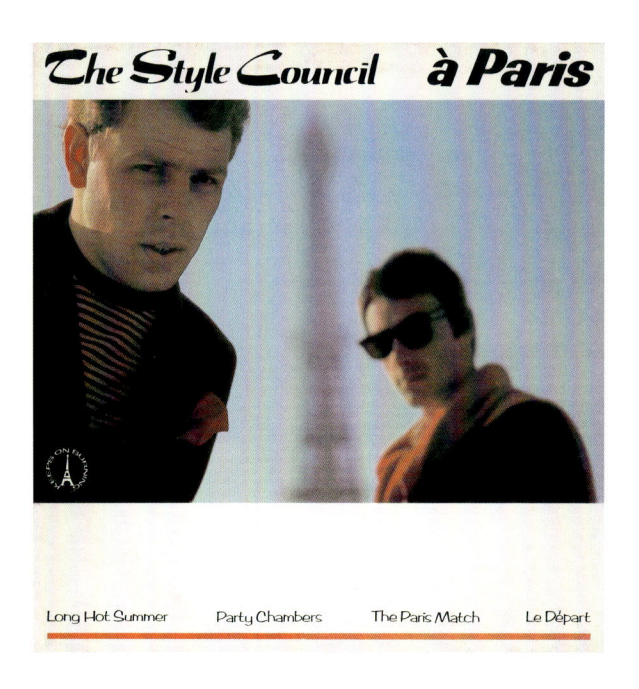

After The Style Council's demise, which had seen Weller briefly flirting with the acid house look, Weller moved back into a late 1960s Mod sensibility. Bands such as Traffic and early 1970s Isley Brothers alongside artists such as Nick Drake and Neil Young were now his musical signposts. Accordingly his dress sense loosened up, with Weller adopting a late 1960s Steve Marriott look with his longish hair, buttoned tops and leather jacket. Shops such as The Duffer of St George, with its colourful and smart neo-Mod clothing, the eye-catching shoes of Patrick Cox and the use of beads and hippyish tops became essential to his well-being.

With the onset of middle age, Weller has moved towards a sleek look, using designers such as Prada and Margaret Howell to fill his wardrobe. He has also designed a range of clothing for Liam Gallagher's Pretty Green label. Musically, his last two albums, *22 Dreams* and *Wake Up the Nation*, have showed him putting aside his normal strengths – melody, riffs, appealing structures – and experimenting with sounds and textures: refusing to stand still, just like all good Modernists should.

Pick up my guitar and play: Paul Weller on acoustic guitar in 2001

# MY GENERATION

By PETER TOWNSHEND

**recorded by THE WHO** on BRUNSW

ESSEX MUSIC LIMITED

# The Who

This is the story of how Roger Daltrey, a sheet metal worker from Shepherd's Bush, John Entwistle, a tax office clerk from Acton, Pete Townshend, an Ealing art student, and Keith Moon, a Beach Boys fanatic from Wembley, got together to place themselves at the forefront of the Mod movement in the UK. Or is it the story of how a band callously hijacked a youth movement to make their name? You decide.

Their birthplace was Acton County School, where Daltrey, Entwistle and Townshend studied in the late 1950s. The three boys all ended up playing with each other in various bands. In 1964 a friend of Pete's, Richard Barnes (see Books), suggested a name change, and they became The Who. Keith Moon now took over drum duties. Enter Mod hustler Pete Meaden, who not only changed the band's name to The High Numbers but also worked on their image, getting them all to embrace the prevalent Mod look of the day.

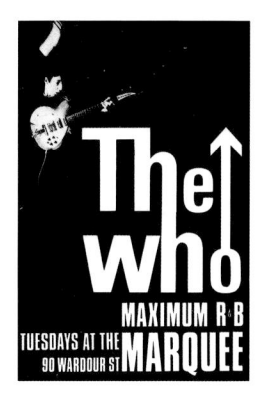

*Opposite:* Sheet music for the 'My Generation' single, 1965

*Top:* The classic poster for the band's 1964 residency at London's Marquee Club

The Who perform at Shepherd's Bush bingo hall in 1964. L to R: John Entwistle, Roger Daltrey, Keith Moon, Pete Townshend

The High Numbers released the Meaden-penned 'I'm The Face' c/w 'Zoot Suit' on the Fontana label, to a distinct lack of interest by the record-buying public. The band were however attracting a steady following of Mods to their regular gigs at The Railway Hotel in Harrow. This venue was where Pete Townshend began smashing up his guitar on stage – by accident at first, later deliberately. In the audience one night were Kit Lambert and Chris Stamp, brother of actor Terence. They bought out Meaden and took over the managerial duties of the band. Pete began to write original material and they signed up with producer Shel Tamy. In late 1964 they reverted to the name The Who and began a residency at The Marquee Club in London's Soho, which they advertised with an iconic black-and-white 'Maximum R'n'B' poster.

January 1965 saw the start of a classic run of Mod-related singles that included 'I Can't

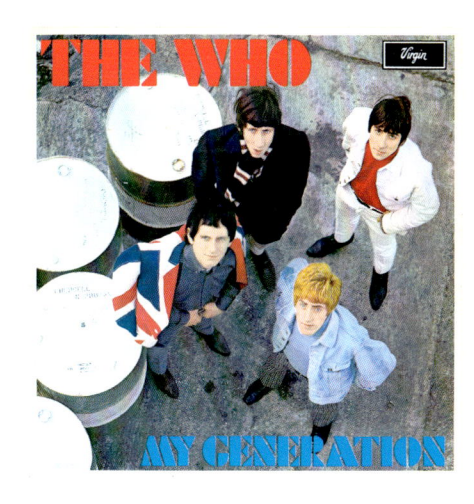

Explain', 'Anyway, Anyhow', 'My Generation', 'Substitute' and 'I Can See For Miles'. Townshend's ability to articulate teenage frustrations aligned with a dynamic songwriting style and caught favour with the London Mod scene, as did albums such as *The Who Sell Out*. By 1969 Mod had changed and the band, thanks to the concept album *Tommy*, had won a huge American audience. However, Mod was deeply embedded in Townshend's psyche and in 1973 he released the double album *Quadrophenia*, another concept album that detailed the adventures of Jimmy, a Shepherd's Bush Mod (see Irish Jack). A film of the album was released in 1979, helping to spark the Mod revival. The band have since staged 'Quadrophenia' concerts and it remains one of their best-loved works.

The 1980 Virgin re-issue of the classic *My Generation* album

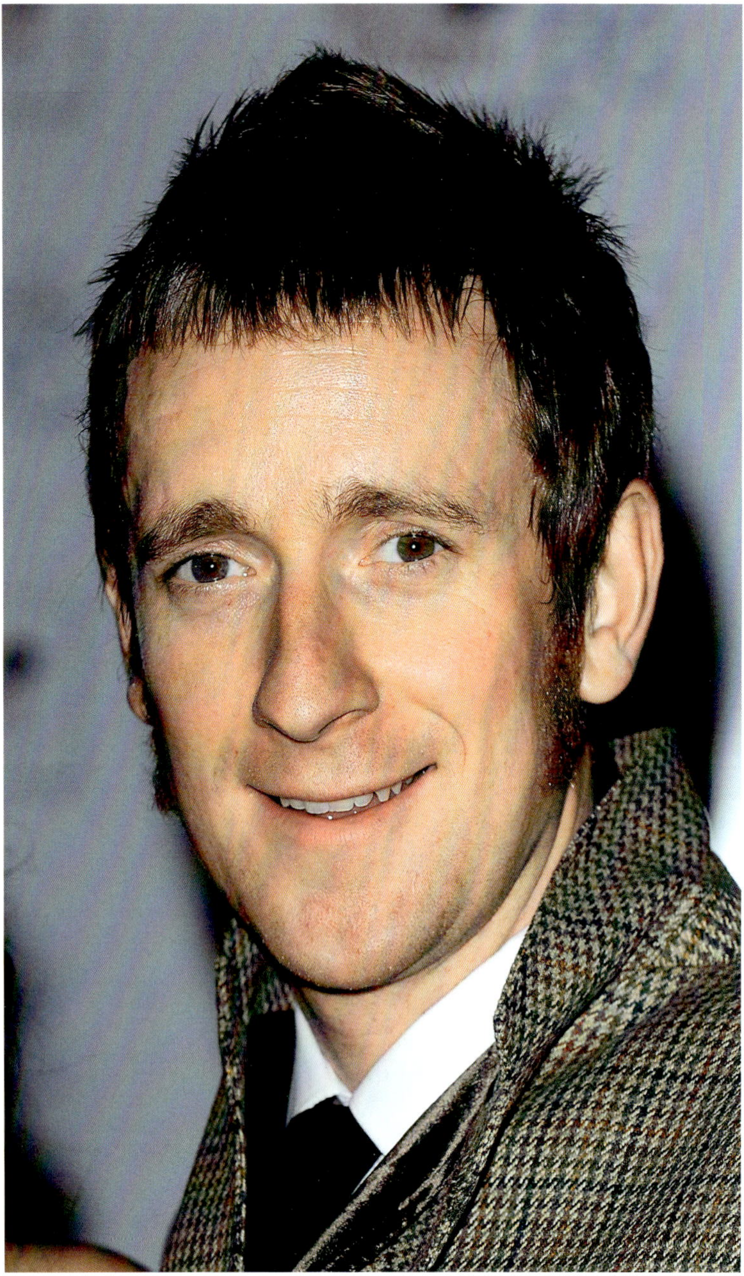

# Bradley Wiggins

A regular question on Mod forum discussion boards is: 'What is the ultimate Mod sport?' The answer is often professional cycling. After all, Mods were the first to wear colourful cycling shirts as a fashion accessory, so it is easy to see why cycling is called the sport of Mods. When a British cyclist was spotted in the run-up to the 2008 Beijing Olympic finals sporting a Mod-style haircut and listening to 'David Watts' by The Jam on his iPod, he suddenly became a figure of great interest to Modernists. Very quickly, he was identified as a high-profile sporting Mod.

Bradley Wiggins was born in Ghent, Belgium, in 1980. His father, Gary, also a cycling professional, was living and training there. Wiggins, however, grew up in London and had his first real exposure to the cycling world at the Herne Hill Velodrome in South London in his early teens. Around the same time he discovered music, developing a high regard for the likes of

*Opposite:* Bradley Wiggins attends the Olympic Gold Ball in London, 2008

*Top:* Bradley Wiggins outside Buckingham Palace after being awarded an CBE by the Prince of Wales at Buckingham Palace, 11 June 2009

In full flow: Wiggins of Team Sky descends on stage 15 of the Tour de France, 2010

The Stone Roses, The Smiths – especially the guitarist Johnny Marr – and Oasis. He was also a big fan of Ocean Colour Scene and in particular their huge hit single, 'The Riverboat Song'. He later went on to discover the work of Paul Weller, with the album *Stanley Road* finding much favour. Backtracking from there, he became aware of The Jam. Alongside all this, Wiggins developed a passionate love of vintage guitars and has become a decent player in the process. He also has a serious shoe fetish, with particular interest in brogues. Reportedly he owns over 40 pairs. He is often spotted 'off duty' in the fashions of Paul Smith, who was a serious cyclist before an accident turned his attention to designing clothes.

The favourite item of clothing in the Wiggins collection is the 'Wiggins Casino' cycling top designed by Milltag, which has Northern Soul-style patches on it. Only 30 of these were made, and sold out instantly.

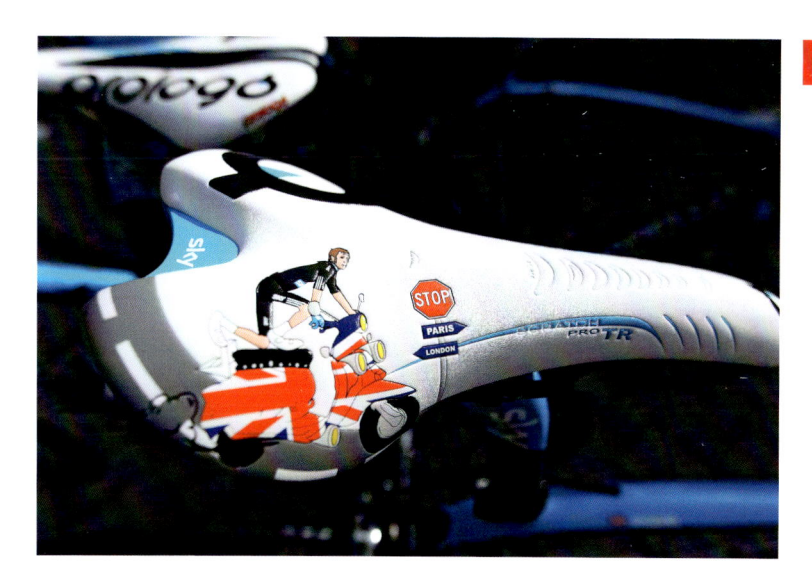

Surprisingly for some, Wiggins revealed that it was in fact John Entwistle, bass player of The Who, and not Paul Weller, who was his idol. He has cited the 1973 *Quadrophenia* album by The Who as a particular favourite. Wiggins is also a big fan of classic 1960s Mod bands The Small Faces, The Kinks and The Who. He has also owned one scooter and has promised himself more.

Wiggins keeps up to date on the music scene in the UK, and mentions The Moons and The Rifles as being among his current listening choices. So there you have it: perhaps the only genuine Mod at the top level in sport, and he's a cyclist. Some would call that fate.

Leaving no one in doubt about his love of all things Mod, Wiggins's customised bike saddle at the 2010 Tour de France

# Generation X

A 1965 book written by journalists Charles Hamblett and Jane Deverson, *Generation X* detailed the lives of the youths of Britain. The interviews, conducted by Deverson, were originally commissioned by the magazine *Woman's Own*. The story they revealed of a generation of Mod teenagers enjoying sex before marriage, experimenting with drugs and having little respect for the older generation so shocked the magazine's editor that he declined to print it. However, Deverson knew she was onto something and she and Hamblett turned their findings into a populist social study which revealed the cultural revolution taking place in Britain. To the public, still recovering from the austerity of the postwar years, the book was very disturbing, but this didn't stop it becoming a bestseller, with John Lennon rumoured to be interested in turning it into a musical. In 1976 a punk band, Generation X, was formed by Billy

Book jacket of the *Generation X* paperback by Charles Hamblett and Jane Deverson

Idol and named in homage to the book, a copy of which was owned by his mother. The singer-songwriter Simon Wells also used one of the book's famous lines about a teenager rotting every night in a coffee bar in a spoken song on his album *Sometimes in the Morning*.

*Top:* The punk band named after the book, featuring Billy Idol (far left)

*Bottom:* Record cover of *Sometimes in the Morning* by Simon Wells

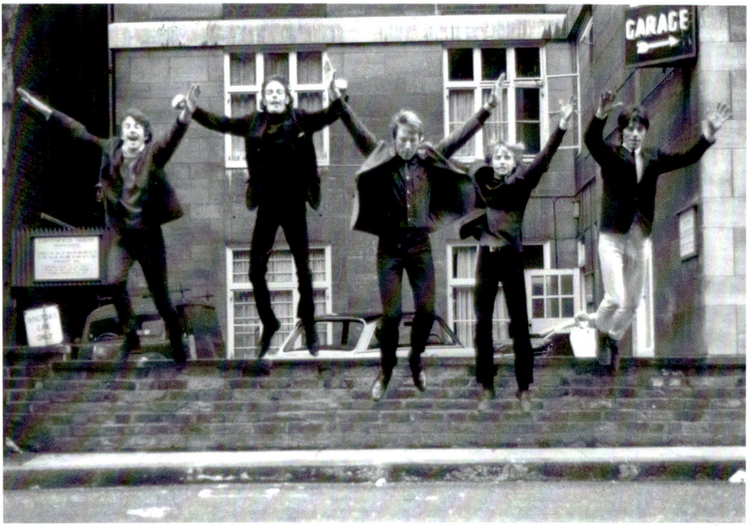
GARAGE

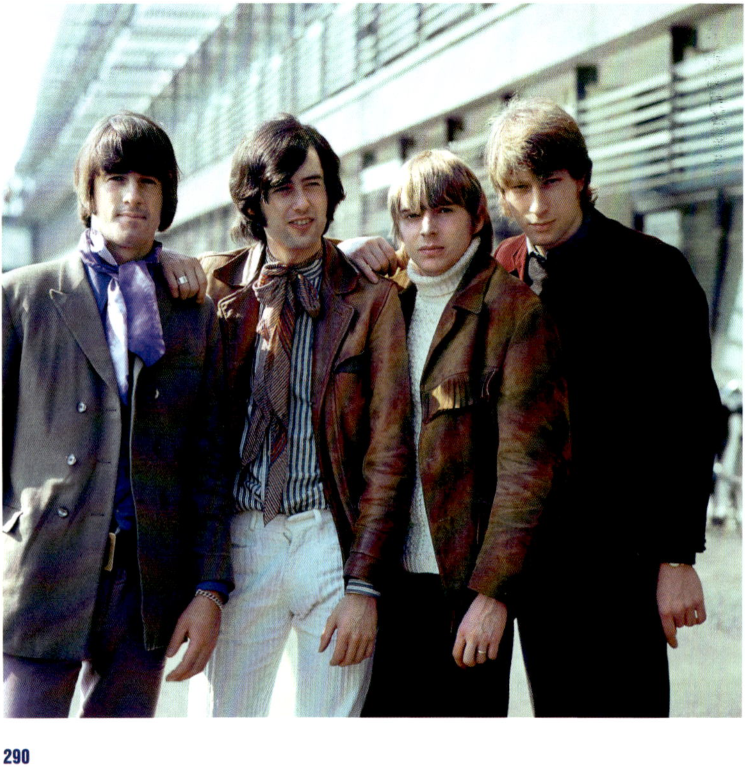

# The Yardbirds

Musically, The Yardbirds divide opinion. Some believe that a band which at some point contained Eric Clapton, Jimmy Page and Jeff Beck in its ranks must by definition be a premier outfit. Others think that very little of their promise was ever really fulfilled. One thing, however, is in no doubt – the band's clothes and great hairstyles automatically lift them into Mod stardom. The Yardbirds existed from 1963 until 1968 and their varying clothes mark the changes of the years, moving from a formal smart jacket and tie look to a more casual style, marked by Keith Relf's long bouffant-styled haircut. They hit the charts a few times, most notably with 'For Your Love', but that old devil called musical differences tore the band apart. Their sense of style, though, always remained intact.

*Opposite top:* The Yardbirds, *circa* late 1965. L to R: drummer Jim McCarthy, bass player Paul Samwell, guitarist Chris Dreja, singer Keith Relf, lead guitarist Jeff Beck

*Opposite bottom:* The Yardbirds, *circa* 1967

# Young Disciples

With their debut album *Road to Freedom* (1991), Young Disciples created a landmark work whose artistic success is strongly linked to a discreet Mod sensibility. The band came together when Femi Williams and Mark Nelson, two huge James Brown fanatics, promoted a Bobby Byrd concert at the Town and Country Club in London's Kentish Town. There they met Carleen Anderson, daughter of James Brown singer Vicki Anderson. Anderson's great vocal ability persuaded Williams and Nelson to join forces. They signed to Gilles Peterson's Talkin' Loud label and – using guest musicians such as ex-James Brown sidemen Maceo Parker and Fred Wesley along with rappers such as IG Culture – put together an album that utilised all aspects of London club culture, from rap to rare groove, from jazz to soul, from past to future. Their songs were subtle and the sound they sculpted was far removed from all their contemporaries. Their smart

*Opposite top:* Marco Nelson, Femi Williams and Carleen Anderson receive an award from legendary Beatles producer George Martin in the early 1990s casual clothing and cool outlook derived from natural Mod instincts. Their single 'Apparently Nothin' hit the top 20 but such attention proved unsatisfactory to Williams and Nelson. They backed out, leaving Anderson to pursue a solo career. Williams and Nelson, in true Mod style, continue to work away from the spotlight.

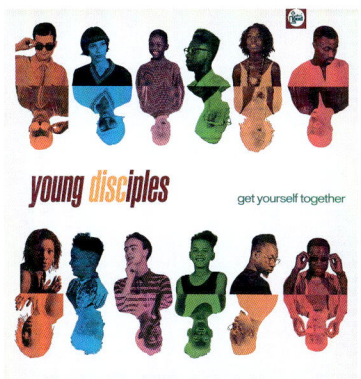

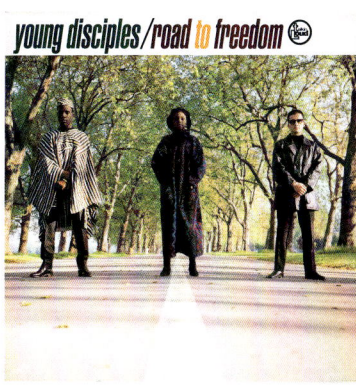

*Bottom left:* Sleeve for the 'Get Yourself Together' 12" single

*Bottom right:* Album cover of *Road to Freedom*, paying homage to those classic Blue Note designs from the 1950s and 1960s

# Zoot Money

Zoot in early 1964

In the mid-1950s a choirboy named George Bruno Money, with a talent for the French horn, heard Ray Charles and Jerry Lee Lewis and changed his life around. He moved onto keyboards and by 1960 had developed a Hammond organ style that was totally unique. Thanks to a Zoot Sims concert he witnessed, George changed his name and began putting together a group, which he named Zoot Money's Big Roll Band. Their rendering of rhythm and blues classics in an impassioned style and Zoot's overt showmanship quickly marked his outfit out from so many others playing similar music. The word spread and soon Mods were packing his gigs at venues such as The Flamingo. Never as sophisticated as Georgie Fame, Zoot's band packed a huge punch and thanks to his wild showmanship was fondly regarded by all. One of Zoot's loyal sidemen was future Police guitarist Andy Summers.

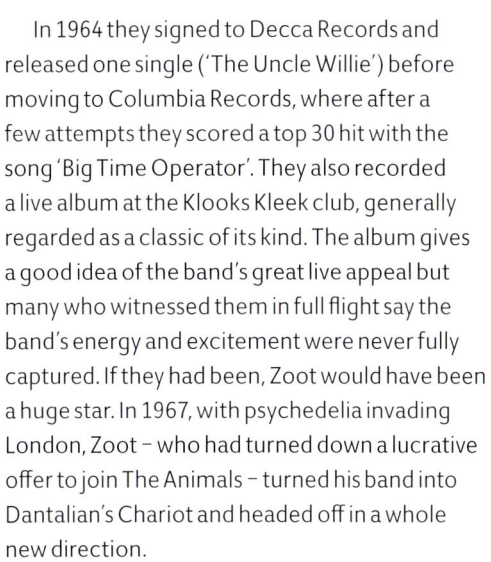

In 1964 they signed to Decca Records and released one single ('The Uncle Willie') before moving to Columbia Records, where after a few attempts they scored a top 30 hit with the song 'Big Time Operator'. They also recorded a live album at the Klooks Kleek club, generally regarded as a classic of its kind. The album gives a good idea of the band's great live appeal but many who witnessed them in full flight say the band's energy and excitement were never fully captured. If they had been, Zoot would have been a huge star. In 1967, with psychedelia invading London, Zoot – who had turned down a lucrative offer to join The Animals – turned his band into Dantalian's Chariot and headed off in a whole new direction.

*Left:* Zoot Money and members of his Big Roll Band

*Right:* Zoot at the Hammond in 1966

# Acknowledgements and Credits

PH: I want to thank all the young Mods of St John the Baptist School, Woking, who in 1971 gave me the picture that has never left me.

For Sahika, The Detail Girl.

MB: This book is for my Lou. The kindness and love you give me every day makes me one lucky man x

Much love to my mentor, colleague and above all friend, Paolo H of the frozen North. *Grazie mille* for the foreword Mr F.

To Andrew Hansen, Philippa Hurd, Martha Jay and all at Prestel, especially my two trainee Modettes, Supriya Malik and our editor Ali Gitlow.

Thanks to Rick and Martina at Getty and especially to all those who have educated me in the ways of Mod over the past 30 years – among them and in no particular order – David Rosen, Fred The Shoe, Little Dave, Eddie P, Bro' Miko, Gorgeous Georgie Dyer, PW, Stevie Ellis, Smiler's one and two, Johnny C, Dave Edwards, DJC, Si Wells, Pete Challis, Chrissy Dolan, Deano Powell, John Simon, The Duffer Chaps, Kev Lock, Phil Dias, Darren Lock, Gary Malby, Raoul Shah, Terry Rawlings, Guy Joseph, Richard Barnes, J de V and GC the knobbly knee.

Huge thanks to the following for trawling through their archives: *Absolute Beginners* - Original cover image © Roger Mayne, Courtesy of Glitterman Gallery; Acid Jazz Records – Eddie Piller, Richard and Ben; Baracuta's G-9 Jacket – Kevin Stone, Craig and Josie; Bass Weejuns – Lesa Wright McHale; Ben Sherman – Daphne Sherman; Blue Note – Markus Evans; Books – Danny @

penpress.co.uk; Brooks Brothers – Chanel de Kock; Clarks - The Alfred Gillett Trust; Clubs Past – Graham Lentz, Mr Jeffrey Kruger; Clubs Present – Paul Welsby, Neil Henderson and Mike Warburton, Baz and Den @ Pip! Pip! Design! and Rob, Paul Tunkin; Randy Cozens – Terry Cozens and Eddie Piller; DC Fontana – Mark Mortimer; Roger Eagle – Paul Welsby and Brian Smith, Geoff and Christine Obrey; The Eyes – Paul 'Smiler' Anderson; Fanzines – Jennie and Colin Baillie, Adam Cooper, Eddie Piller; Fleur De Lys – Paul 'Smiler' Anderson; Fred Perry – Reuben Billingham, Natalia and Lola; Dave Godin – Ady Croasdell; Irish Jack – Jack Lyons, Seamus Murphy, Dave Wyburn and Tetsuro Hirano; The Isle of Wight Scooter Rally- Dave Edwards; The Ivy Shop – John Simon and Andy; James Taylor Quartet – Eddie, Ben and Richard at Acid Jazz; Jump the Gun – Jonathan and Adam Le Roy; Kent Records – Ady Croasdell; Levi's Jeans– Carlos Williams; Mohair – George Dyer, Stuart and Lucy Murray at Ace Face Clothing; Northern Soul – Ady Croasdell; Online Modernists – Thierry Steuve, Sarah Bolshi, Lloyd Johnson and David Walker; Peckham Rye – Martin Brighty and David Walker; *Quadrophenia - The Film* – Sue Armstrong @ Universal; Revival – The Well Suspect, Jeff Shadbolt, Alex Deverill, Tracey Wilmot, Buddy Ascott; The Scooter – Steve @ VFM, Derry Kunman; Stax Records – Abbey Anna, Wolfgang Frank and Tim Sampson; Stone Foundation – Lee Cogswell, Stone Foundation, Delicious Junction Footwear; Tootal Scarves – David Green, Neal Dawson, Kevin Stone and Phil Dias @ Karma Creative.co.uk; Generation X – Dug Wolfsohn, Rob @ 208 Records and Simon Wells.

The following have been provided by Getty Images:

*Frontispiece* Popperfoto/Contributor; Contents David Redfern/Staff; *p. 5* David Redfern/Staff; *p. 7* Gareth Cattermole/Staff; *p. 11* Peter Dunne/Stringer; *p. 12* Popperfoto/Contributor; *p. 14* Georges DeKeerle/Contributor; *p. 15* Jill Fromer; *p. 23* Petra Niemeier-K and K/Contributor; *p. 24* TRBfoto; *p. 25* Nick Veasey; *p. 26* Burton Berinsky/Contributor; *p. 27* top and bottom: Blank Archives/Contributor; *p. 28* GAB Archive/Contributor; *p. 29* Michael Ochs Archives/Stringer; *p. 31* top: Michael Ochs Archives/Stringer; bottom: Ron Howard/Contributor; *p. 42* top left and right: GAB Archive/Contributor; bottom: Brian Shuel/Contributor; *pp. 44-45* Michael Ochs Archives/Stringer; *p. 48* Gered Mankowitz/Contributor; *p. 51* Michel Linssen/Contributor; *p. 53* Tim Roney/Contributor; *p. 56* Getty Images/Staff; *p. 57* Walter Daran/Contributor; *p. 58* Hulton Archive/Stringer; *p. 59* Pictorial Parade/Staff; *p. 60* Jon Furniss/Contributor; *pp. 61-62* GAB Archive/Contributor; *p. 63* Jeremy Fletcher/Contributor; *p. 64* bottom and *p. 65* top left: GAB Archive/Contributor; *p. 65* top right: Robert Knight Archive/Contributor; *p. 66* left: Popperfoto/Contributor; *p. 67* Royal Photographic Society/Contributor; *p. 70* Michael Ochs Archives/Stringer; *p. 73* David Redfern/Staff; *p. 74* Jeremy Fletcher/Contributor; *p. 75* Leon Morris/Contributor; *p. 76* Roy Jones/Stringer; *p. 78* Keystone Features/Stringer; *p. 95* Petra Niemeier- K and K/Contributor; *p. 100* David Redfern/Staff; *p. 101* left: Sylvia Pitcher/Contributor; *p. 108* Keystone/Stringer; *p. 118* Ferdaus Shamim/Contributor; *p. 119* Simon James/Contributor; *p. 121* Tim Hall/Contributor; *p. 123* CA/Staff; *p. 124* Fiona Adams/Contributor; *p. 127* Erica Echenberg/Contributor; *p. 128* GAB Archive/Contributor; *p. 132* Silver Screen Collection/Contributor; *p. 134* M. Mckeown/Stringer; *p. 135* Universal Images Group/Contributor; *p. 144* John Hoppy Hopkins/Contributor; *p. 146* top: David Redfern/Staff; *p. 147* top: John Hoppy Hopkins/Contributor; bottom: Michael Ochs Archives/Stringer; *p. 155* Bloomberg/Contributor; *p. 157* Archive Photos/Stringer; *p. 158* R. McPhedran/Stringer; *p. 159* Keystone/Stringer; *p. 160* Ronald Dumont/Stringer; *p. 161* Popperfoto/Contributor; *p. 165* Michael Ochs Archives/Stringer; *p. 168* Charlie Gillett Collection/Contributor; *p. 170* Michael Ochs Archives/Stringer; *p. 171* Bob Parent/Contributor; *p. 174* top: GAB Archive/Contributor; bottom: Michael Ochs Archives/Stringer; *p. 175* Gilles Petard/Contributor; *p. 176* GAB Archive/Contributor; *p. 177* Archive Photos/Stringer; *p. 178* Frank Driggs Collection/Contributor; *p. 180* Main and *p. 182*: Mick Gold/Contributor, *p. 189* Terry Disney/Stringer; *p. 190* Central Press/Stringer; *p. 191* Bruce Fleming/Contributor; *p. 192* Diverse Images; *p. 193* Larry Ellis/Stringer; *p. 194* Paul Popper/Popperfoto/Contributor; *p. 195* top: Keystone/Stringer; bottom: Keystone; *p. 202* John Loengard/Contributor; *pp. 203–05* Tony Evans/Timelapse Library Ltd./Contributor; *p. 207* Central Press/Stringer; *p. 208* Jeremy Fletcher/Contributor; *p. 209* GAB Archive/Contributor; *p. 210* Keystone/Stringer; *p. 211* Rolls Press/Popperfoto; *p. 212* Bob Thomas/Contributor; *p. 213* Evening Standard/Stringer; *p. 214* Peter Francis/Contributor; *p. 216* left: Michael Ochs Archives/Stringer; right: David Refern/Staff; *p. 217* BIPS/Stringer; *p. 218* Fin Costello/Staff; *p. 225* Chris Morphet/Contributor; *p. 226* David Redfern/Staff; *p. 227* top: Ian Dickson/Contributor; bottom: Nigel Osbourne/Contributor; *p. 228* bottom: Bruno Vincent/Staff; *p. 229* top left: Fox Photos/Stringer; bottom right: Chad Buchanan/Stringer; *p. 230* Terrence Spencer/Contributor; *p. 231* bottom: Apic/Contributor; *p. 232* top and bottom: Popperfoto/Contributor; *p. 233* top: William H. Alden/Stringer; *p. 235* top: Andrew H. Walker/Stringer; *p. 238* Ivan Keeman/Contributor; *p. 239* Petra Niemeier-K and K/Contributor; *p. 240* M. McKeown/Stringer; *p. 242* Michael Ochs Archives/Handout; *p. 244* Charlie Gillett Collection/Contributor; *p. 245* Michael Ochs Archives/Stringer; *p. 246* Blank Archives/Contributor; *p. 249* Michael Ochs Archives/Stringer; *p. 252* Petra Niemeier- K and K/Contributor; *pp. 254–55* Terrence Spencer/Contributor; *p. 262* Popperfoto/Contributor; *p. 264* M. McKeown/Stringer; *p. 265* Popperfoto/Contributor; *p. 266* Caroline Greville-Morris/Contributor; *p. 267* Jill Douglas/Contributor; *p. 268* John White/Stringer; *p. 269* Chris Morphet/Contributor; *p. 271* left: Popperfoto/Contributor; *p. 274* Steve Morley/Staff; *p. 277* Ebet Roberts/Contributor; *p. 279* Peter Pakvis/Contributor; *p. 281* GAB Archive/Contributor; *p. 282* Michael Ochs Archive/Stringer; *p. 284* Eamonn McCormack/Contributor; *p. 285* WPA Pool/Pool; *pp. 286–87* Bryn Lennon/Staff; *p. 289* top: Gered Mankowitz; *p. 290* top: John Pratt/Stringer; bottom: Jan Persson/Contributor; *p. 293* top: Mick Hutson/Contributor; *p. 294* Jeremy Fletcher/Contributor; *p. 295* left: GAB Archive/Contributor; right: David Redfern/Staff; *p. 301* Mike McLaren/Stringer; *p. 303* Virginia Turbett/Contributor; *p. 304* Dwight Eschliman.

**299**

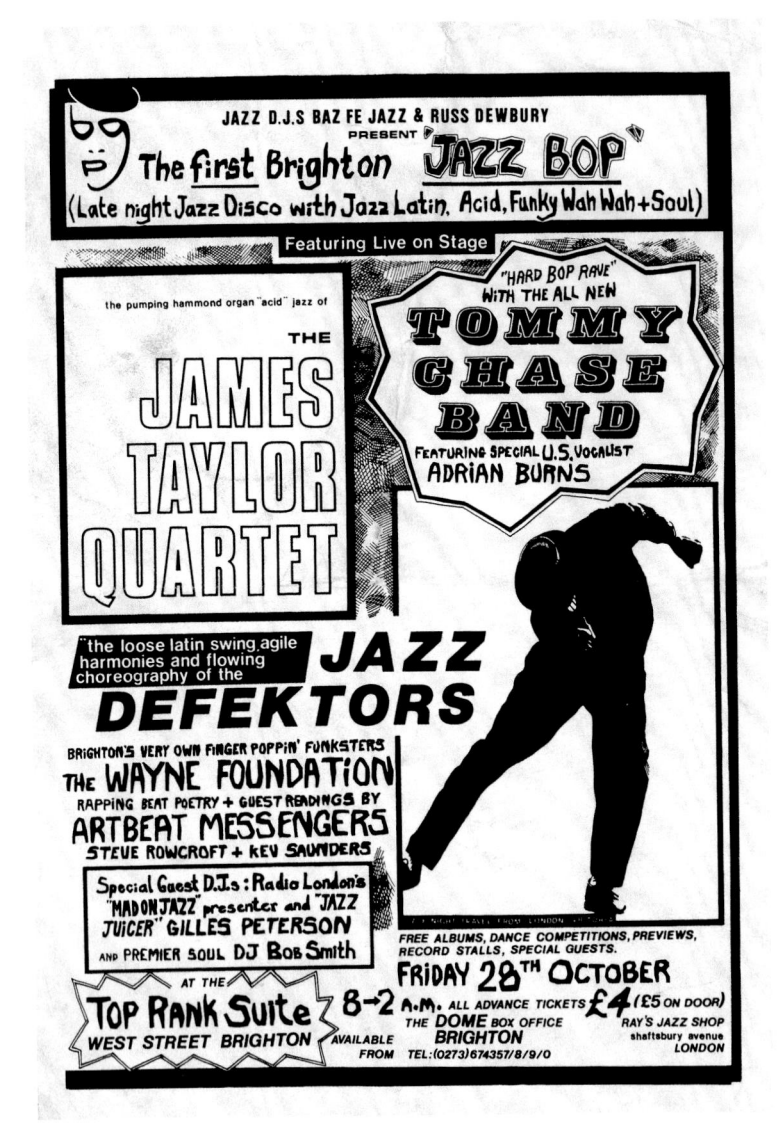

A flyer from the first Brighton
Jazz Bop from October 1988 –
Neo Mod Central!

Two girls dancing to the Northern Soul sounds at The Moonlight Club, London, in 1979

© For the text by Paolo Hewitt and Mark Baxter, 2012

© For illustrations see Acknowledgements and Credits, page 296

The rights of Paolo Hewitt and Mark Baxter to be identified as authors of this work have been asserted in accordance with the Copyright, Designs and Patents Act 1988.

*Front cover:* see illustrations on pages 29, 32, 36, 66, 73, 161, 174, 194, 217, 228, 259, 264

*Frontispiece:* The best-dressed member of The Rolling Stones, drummer Charlie Watts, in 1964

*Back cover:* see illustrations on pages 100, 119, 150, 174, 232, 235

**Prestel, a member of Verlagsgruppe Random House GmbH**

**Prestel Verlag**
Neumarkter Str. 28
81673 Munich
Tel. +49 (0)89 4136-0
Fax +49 (0)89 4136-2335
www.prestel.de

**Prestel Publishing Ltd.**
4 Bloomsbury Place
London WC1A 2QA
Tel. +44 (0)20 7323-5004
Fax +44 (0)20 7636-8004
www.prestel.com

**Prestel Publishing**
900 Broadway, Suite 603
New York, NY 10003
Tel. +1 (212) 995-2720
Fax +1 (212) 995-2733
www.prestel.com

Library of Congress Control Number: 2011944329

British Library Cataloguing-in-Publication Data: a catalogue record for this book is available from the British Library; the Deutsche Nationalbibliothek holds a record of this publication in the Deutsche Nationalbibliografie; detailed bibliographical data can be found under: http://dnb.d-nb.de

Prestel books are available worldwide. Please contact your nearest bookseller or one of the above addresses for information concerning your local distributor.

*Editorial direction* Ali Gitlow
*Editorial assistance* Supriya Malik
*Copyedited by* Martha Jay
*Production* Friederike Schirge
*Design and layout* Sugarfree
*Origination* Reproline Mediateam, Munich
*Printing and binding* APPL aprinta druck GmbH & Co. KG, Wemding

*Printed in Germany*

FSC
www.fsc.org
MIX
Paper from responsible sources
FSC® C004592

Verlagsgruppe Random House
FSC-DEU-0100

The FSC®-certified paper Hello Silk has been supplied by Deutsche Papier.

ISBN: 978-3-7913-4605-2

Leaving on a jet plane: Model Twiggy and her then partner and manager Justin de Villeneuve fly off to sunnier climes in 1968

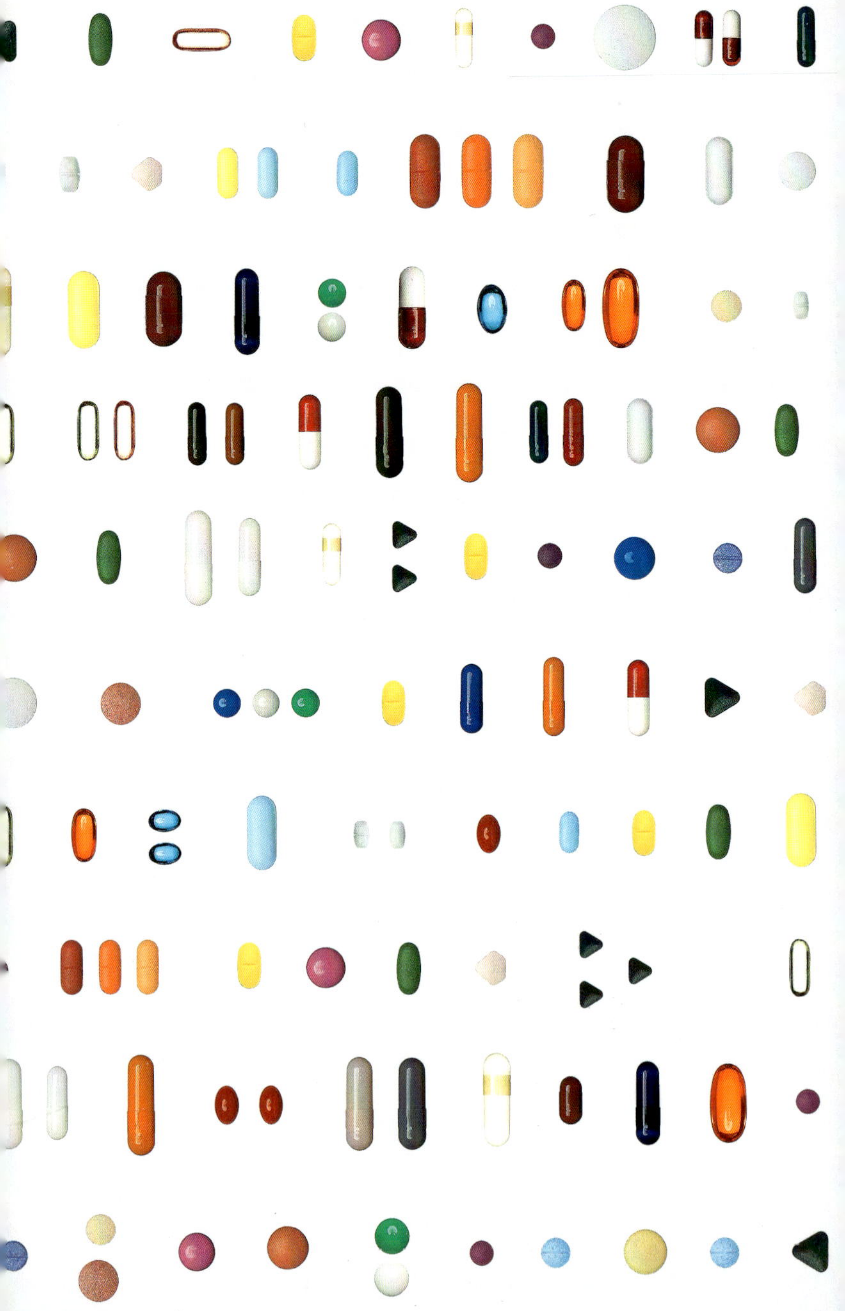